For Joe – I had some fun
with the Admiral while
editing this one – he felt
he had to protect the family
name so I couldn't quite
tell the truth about his
favorite Uncle – who was a
bit inclined to stretch the blanket –

Jeff

THE WESTERN FRONTIER LIBRARY

(For a complete list, see page 201.)

THE WEST OF THE TEXAS KID

THE WEST OF TH

TEXAS KID, 1881—1910

Recollections of

THOMAS EDGAR CRAWFORD

COWBOY

GUN FIGHTER

RANCHER

HUNTER

MINER

Edited and with an Introduction by
JEFF C. DYKES

With Original Drawings by
Nick Eggenhofer

Norman

UNIVERSITY OF OKLAHOMA PRESS

LIBRARY OF CONGRESS CATALOG CARD NUMBER: 62–10768

Copyright 1962 by the University of Oklahoma Press,
Publishing Division of the University.
Composed and printed at Norman, Oklahoma, U.S.A.,
by the University of Oklahoma Press.
First edition.

To my friends who have gone,
"Adios" till the Last Roundup.

INTRODUCTION

"THE TEXAS KID" was only one of the names that Thomas Edgar Crawford answered to in the West. He was also called "The Montana Kid," "Buckskin," "Kid," and "Ed." He dictated a highly entertaining narrative. It was written in 1938 when he was over seventy, and he failed to make use of the standard historical references to check his recollections. As one of his nephews, a high-ranking officer in our Department of Defense, now retired, told this writer: "My uncle wrote the truth as closely as he could recall it. I heard him tell many of these experiences and stories when as a boy I stayed with him on his Montana ranch. He was my mother's brother. He was no more than five feet, six inches tall, with gray eyes and brown hair, and quite wiry. I kept in touch with him from 1898 until he died in 1941. He probably weighed about 140 pounds when I first visited him at the Meagher County ranch, but as he got older, he became even thinner. He was deeply tanned. He married twice—his first wife died in Montana many years ago, but his second wife, the mother of his two daughters, is still living."

Crawford invested the money from the sale of his California mine in Florida real estate, including an orange grove. His large home located at the citrus orchard burned down shortly after he moved in. It was then that he built the log house mentioned in his foreword.

Crawford did not always stay in Florida after establishing his home there about 1910–12. In 1918–19 he investigated the gold fields of Costa Rica for Minor C. Keith and Associates of New York City. He also looked over the country for tropical woods having possible commercial value. He spent much of his time in the rain forests and had many thrilling adventures with game, including killing a *Tigre Grande* (next to the Bengal in size) with a six-shooter. Crawford had made a previous pleasure trip to Honduras and was not a stranger to the ways of the tropical jungle. In Honduras he met Lee Christmas, put on a rough-riding demonstration for the natives, and hunted deer and tigers.

The same mining syndicate that Crawford represented in Costa Rica sent him on a prospecting trip to British Columbia and Alaska in June, 1919. He spent the winter of 1919–20 in Alaska, examining a number of claims owned by the syndicate and trying to locate other likely ore deposits. He traveled by dog sled and on snowshoes over a wide territory that winter. He renewed his acquaintance with the bear tribe, but was apparently too busy to hunt very much. Crawford wrote that he was glad to get back to Florida after his winter in the frozen north.

In editing this manuscript, I have made no attempt to reconstruct the sentences—Crawford had his own way of telling things. That way, while not always grammatically correct, constitutes part of the strength of the narrative. Some corrections in spelling have been made, but this is Crawford's story as he dictated it. In dictating it, he was sometimes repetitious and in many cases he recalled and added details about certain happenings that he had previously covered. So far as possible, the material on a particular subject or incident has been gathered in one place in this book. The clearest, most forceful versions of those happenings duplicated in the dictation have been selected, and the others eliminated.

Checking out the people, places, dates, and happenings included in the Crawford narrative proved to be an impossible task. As a matter of fact, Crawford did not specifically mention very many dates, but he did include some incidents that are easy to date. In the early part of the narrative he was dictating from memory about happenings over half a century in the past—and time does dim the memory. In one chapter he referred to George Curry as "Big Nose George," but in another chapter he called him "Flat Nose George." Since it was obvious that the man he knew was Flat Nose George Curry, the text was corrected. Big Nose George Parrot (sometimes called Curry), train robber and killer, was hanged by the vigilantes in Rawlins, Wyoming, in 1881, the year Crawford started west.

In a number of cases there is a strong suspicion that Crawford was stretching the blanket some, perhaps to the tearing point. For example, the tale of Belle Starr's joining Crawford and Henry Starr on a long, roundabout saddle trip from Laredo, Texas, to Indian Territory (Oklahoma) in the middle eighties is hard to swallow. Crawford identifies Henry Starr as the bank robber and says Henry was a couple of years older than himself. According to the generally accepted authorities, Crawford was six years older than Starr (Crawford was born in 1867 and Starr in 1873). Crawford says Belle was about thirteen years older than Henry, but this is also incorrect. According to her biographers, Belle was born in 1846 (some say 1848), making her twenty-seven years older than Henry. This was one of the occasions when Crawford was a little vague about time, but as near as can be figured from his saga the journey must have taken place about 1884 or 1885. If this is right, Belle was thirty-eight or -nine and Henry a mere lad of eleven or twelve. Crawford implies that Henry and Belle were lovers and wonders if they ever married. If Crawford made this saddle trip with Belle, it is apparent that Henry Starr, the notorious robber who was killed while holding up the bank at Harrison, Arkansas, in 1921, was not the third member of the party. It could have been another Henry Starr or another Henry or another Starr, or maybe Crawford simply felt that the introduction of such characters as Belle Starr and Henry Starr would spice up his narrative.

An examination of a considerable amount of material on Thomas (Black Jack) Ketchum in this writer's collection of Outlawiana fails to reveal any mention of Kid Crawford or The Texas Kid. This is not to say they didn't team up as Crawford claims. The period in which Crawford says that they rode and worked together as cowboys precedes the time that Ketchum really turned outlaw. Most authorities agree that it was in the early nineties (some say 1892) that Ketchum got into serious trouble with the law in the Southwest. By that time Crawford had been "working" out of Jackson Hole for several years. It is possible that Ketchum entered the Hole with Crawford and served an apprenticeship with the "Train Robbers Syndicate" (a term also applied to the Wild Bunch), as the Jackson Hole outlaws were tabbed by a magazine writer many years later. It has been generally thought that Ketchum was just a hard-working cowboy before he and his brother Sam recruited a small gang to hold up his first train in New Mexico. Perhaps the real explanation is

xii

that Ketchum, tired of the North country, returned to the Southwest. It is possible that Black Jack and Crawford worked for the Hash Knife in Arizona, but not while Burt Mossman was the manager. Cap took over the management in 1898 after Crawford had started ranching in Montana.

Crawford does not openly admit that he killed even a single white man or that he ever participated in a train or bank robbery. This is probably explained by the brief statement in his foreword—"If I were a bachelor, I might write you a more lively tale. But I have a wife and two little girls, and, as you know, children need protection." However, in this writer's opinion he all but says that he was the "John" of the trio that robbed the Utah bank in Chapter 10. Crawford admits he earned quite a reputation while he was a long rider, but he carefully avoids telling exactly *how* he earned it. Despite his reluctance to discuss frankly his own roles, he provides considerable material on both the Jackson Hole and the Hole in the Wall outlaws.

He was a man of rather strong feelings—he liked horses and he didn't like sheep—he could understand a train or bank robber, but more than once took the trail after a horse thief. After he settled down to ranching in Montana, he helped to send up some cow thieves. He loved to hunt, and some of his best stories are about his adventures with game. He felt that the Montana horse and the Montana cowboy were unequalled anywhere and that the manner of handling a roundup on the northern plains was superior to the way it was done on the southern plains. Some will say he was just plain prejudiced. But in his strong presentation of his opinions he has preserved much lore and perhaps added some to the legends of his West. His story is presented not as history, but as one man's recollections (at times, obviously in error) of the West as he knew it.

CONTENTS

PART III

Ranching in Montana, 1896–1905

PART IV

Death Valley Ways, 1906–10

FOREWORD

I AM LIVING THE LIFE of the average citizen. My house is
a good big log cabin on the edge of St. Andrews Bay, Florida. I feel more at home in it than I do in a modern house.
There are years of "gathering" strung around the walls. A
few of the articles are: grass pack-bags and machetes from
the tropics (the bags are stained with the blood of red mon-
keys that were shot for food while I was in the jungle of
Costa Rica); rifle, shotguns, six-shooter, and belt; rawhide
rope and spurs, all from the West. From Alaska came snowshoes, prospecting pick, horn spoon, gold pan, knives and
compass, two buckskin shirts decorated with bear claws and
elk teeth, moosehide moccasins, mittens, and pack saddles.
These and many other souvenirs tell me tales.

On the floors and walls are skins of fur-bearing animals
and of reptiles which abound in this visinity, that I have
trapped and shot. These are bear, whitetail deer, bobcat,
coon, gray fox, alligator, rattlesnake, skunk, and opossum.
Tackle suitable for fresh-water or deep-sea fishing is in
place too.

It's just my nature to bring the results of the chase or

the hunt home and throw them on the floor or have them on the walls. They seem to make it more homelike. I never consulted any interior decorator to tell how to do it. The size of the living room is twenty-two by thirty-three feet. The dining room is the same.

I hold no grudges. I have always had friends. My friends were of all kinds and from all walks of life. I treat all men square and wish every one well that I know. If I were a bachelor, I might write you a more lively tale. But I have a wife and two little girls, and, as you know, children need protection.

I have been accused of things I never did, and I have done things that never got into print. I was young and full of pep. My companions were rough. There was no one to say "No." I offer no apologies. I belong to no church, but I believe in a Supreme Being and respect all religions.

THOMAS EDGAR CRAWFORD

PART I

Saddle Tramp Days, 1881–87

CHAPTER ONE

OHIO WAS TOO TAME FOR ME

I WAS BORN in northern Ohio in 1867, and I guess I had a little of the wild born in me. On my father's side I was related to Captain Jack Crawford, the "Poet Scout." My grandfather on my mother's side was last seen by his family when he walked away from home with only his gun and his dog. He wore a wolfskin cap with the teeth in front and the tail hanging down behind, and was headed north. The settlement had become too dense for him; that settlement is now part of the city of Lansing, Michigan, then a part of their homestead.

About as far back as I can remember I was trapping such game as muskrat, mink, skunk, and other fur-bearing animals. The first gun I ever owned that would shoot powder and shot I made myself. The barrel was about a foot long, and was made out of a piece of hollow lightning rod. I pounded one end flat, bent it over and bound it to a wooden stock that was made very much like the old Cross gunstock. The sights were on top of the stock at the side of the barrel, the rear sight being about a foot back of the breech. This gave considerable distance between the front and the rear

3

sight. Near the breech I bored a touchhole where I would prime it and touch it off with a match scratched on a piece of sandpaper tacked to the side of the stock. The puff of smoke from the priming did not interfere very much with the sighting, and with it I killed chipmunks, rabbits, and some birds.

When I was ten years old I was taking part in all the annual turkey shoots at Thanksgiving and Christmas. I always brought home some turkeys. At this time I owned a .44 rimfire, brass breech, Winchester rifle given me by my friend John High, a hardware dealer in Seville, Ohio. I used this gun in competition with the gray-haired old fellows who shot old muzzle-loader rifles, with set triggers and all kinds of fancy sights, wind gauges, etc. From time to time I owned also several old pistols and was a fairly good shot with them.

The Christmas before I left home, some hunters returned from a trip up in Michigan and got up a shooting match with a black bear as the prize. I set up a three-hundred-yard target, which was the distance they were going to shoot. I had gotten the range down to a nicety, but when the day of the shoot came, the old fellows barred me out on account of my gun, saying that none but the muzzle-loaders were allowed. It strikes me now that I must have been a pretty fair shot at that time to have scared those old fellows.

The gang I ran with was a bunch of young roughnecks. We smoked, chewed tobacco, and drank whisky. I played hooky from school most of the time to go fishing, hunting, or skating and often remained away from home overnight to spend the time along the bank of some creek or in the woods by myself.

Some of the boys in the gang worked in the brewery, and during the week it was their business to roll one or two five-gallon kegs of beer down the slope so as to land among a

4

bunch of empty kegs. After dark it was our business to get them and carry them to the woods; there we had a cave underneath and among the roots of a large elm tree which we used for our Saturday night and Sunday sprees.

Our den was the scene of many a wild night. It was located about a mile and a half from town, in a deep, heavily wooded canyon on Sugar Creek. We had a few cooking utensils and usually one or more stolen chickens. Our time was spent in eating and drinking, and reading such books as *Wild Bill Hickok, Kit Carson, Captain Jack Crawford: The Poet Scout, California Joe* and *Beadle's Dime Novels*.

My twin brother Bert, when he was ten years of age, lost his right foot in a mowing-machine accident. When he recovered, it was his ambition to become a telegrapher. We had an instrument set up in our home and connected it with instruments in the homes of some other boys. While Bert was learning, I learned too and became a fairly good operator. This always helped me later in beating my way on the railroads. I became proficient in getting on and off of moving trains. I was husky and could walk a city block on my hands and do almost all of the stunts that were done in the circuses which visited our town.

One day, a short time before I left Ohio, my mother sent Bert to the butcher shop of Hen Wiler to get some meat and small change. Bert was then walking on a cork foot. When Bert entered the shop, Wiler was waiting on a customer, a tall, rough, half-intoxicated fellow named John Gilmore. It was rumored that Gilmore had killed one man and shot two others.

When Bert asked for small change, Gilmore spoke up: "Of course these boys want small change. They are always stealing money."

"I would like to know who steals more money than your

5

boy," replied my brother, referring to Gilmore's oldest boy, Harry.

Gilmore turned and kicked Bert, knocked him down, and scattered the change all over the floor. Bert quickly gathered himself up, hurried through the door to the street, and picked up a half-brick from the badly worn pavement. When Gilmore came out of the shop the brick met him squarely and hard in the face, knocking him down in turn. I stood near by and saw the trouble; Bert ran for home.

After Gilmore's face had been washed and he had recovered from the shock, he started for his home saying, "I'll be back and clean up them damn brats."

I hurried home, which was only a block away. I got my Winchester rifle, went out through the back yard into the alley, and up the alley to the point where it crossed the street where Gilmore lived. Between the point where I stood in the middle of the road and Gilmore's house, there was a little hollow with a bridge crossing Sugar Creek in the bottom. Gilmore came down the street on the opposite hill, carrying a shotgun. I stood in the road and intended to kill Gilmore as soon as he crossed the bridge. Not knowing the size of shot he intended to shoot, I considered myself within shotgun range. There were a lot of people standing about two hundred feet back of me on Main Street watching us; no one interfered or came near me. Gilmore must have had a hunch, for just before he reached the bridge, he turned back and went home. He did not come to town for several days. The next time I saw him he was sober, and nothing was said about the trouble.

By this time the East was altogether too tame for me; my only ambition was to go West and become a cowboy. In the early spring of 1881 (I was fourteen years old that summer), I climbed into the caboose of a freight train and began the first leg of my journey to the cow country. I knew the conductor and brakeman on the train so was welcome to the ride. My total capital amounted to sixteen dollars that I had received from the sale of skins I had trapped the previous winter. From then on I was, strictly speaking, beating my way and on my own.

One pang of homesickness, I remember very distinctly, came over me on the second day out. I was standing on a bridge in Toledo, Ohio, with a crowd of people watching the ice break up in the Maumee River. It was a cold, raw day with a chilling drizzle of rain. My thoughts turned longingly homeward, but I bucked up when it struck me as an indication of weakness to think of turning back. I had lost my bearings, so I asked a man standing near me the way to a railroad which ran west. I was on my way again.

CHAPTER TWO

COWBOY ON COWSKIN CREEK

I CAME INTO ST. LOUIS, MISSOURI, in the early morning on the top of a passenger coach. I had intended to get down before coming into town, but didn't get a chance. A lot of people saw me climb down at the depot, and among them was a policeman. He beckoned to me, and we left the depot together. He was a kind, fatherly sort of man, and asked me a lot of questions. As we were passing a restaurant I asked him if I could go in and get my breakfast; he consented and we went in together. He questioned me all through the meal.

"Where are you from?"

"Smithville, Ohio," I replied.

"Where are you going?"

"West," I said.

"Do your parents know where you are? What do they do?"

"My father is dead," I answered, "My mother has a dress-making and millinery shop. I am going west to get a job as a telegraph operator. I do not like the East. I am not running away from home; my mother knows all about it." Every word I told him was the truth.

After leaving the restaurant we walked down the street

together for a short distance. Looking up a street, I saw a long red arm at the railroad crossing drop down across the street to halt the traffic. I asked the policeman if the train was going west. He said with a smile that it was. "May I go?" I asked. He looked at me, smiled and said "Yes." I got to the crossing just as the engine was passing; and in spite of the effort of the one-legged gateman to motion me back, I ducked under the bar, caught the blind baggage car and left that town.

In a few days I fetched up in Wichita, Kansas, which was in the midst of a great boom; people stood in line nearly two blocks long at the post office, waiting many hours for the general-delivery mail. The place seemed to have about ten thousand people in it, and there were not enough houses for them all. The streets were filled with people, and from every business house signs stuck out prominently announcing "Real Estate for Sale" or "Abstract and Title Office." Everyone talked real estate, and buying and selling were going on briskly.

Wichita at that time had some kind of a saloon law, and the city was supposed to be dry. However, there was a Bismarck-looking German, who weighed over three hundred pounds, named Fritz Snitzler who controlled or owned a number of blind-tiger saloons scattered all over town. It was no trouble to get liquor.

The last twenty-four hours of my railroad journey into Wichita had been in a carload of coke which cut my clothes into rags and tatters and nearly tore them off me. I presented a fine appearance when I applied for, and got, a job at the Occidental Hotel—a job washing dishes. I was so short that they stood me on a stool in order to reach the washtub. It was not very long, however, before I landed

9

work on the ranch of Mr. H. K. Eberly, located on Cowskin Creek about ten miles west of town.

Cowskin Creek was peculiar in that it was very boggy near the edges, but had a solid bottom in the center. In order to cross with a horse you had to jump him to the center, then jump him to the other bank. Cattle with their big bodies, short legs, big feet and knees, are very good in boggy ground or in quicksand. They will wallow through by crawling on their knees while a horse will rear up and bog down.

The creek was very pretty. It was crooked and lined on each bank with timber, mostly box elder, cottonwood, wild-plum bushes, and other trees which looked good in that prairie country.

Mr. Eberly was a big cattle feeder and bought cattle from all the surrounding country. I was soon going with him on his cattle-buying trips, and was in the saddle most of the time. We went as far west as Dodge City on the Arkansas River and the Old Cimarron Crossing on the Santa Fe Trail. Dodge City was going strong as a cow town. I was fascinated with the hurdy-gurdy houses, gambling and dance halls.

When fall came I started to close herd a bunch of stock cattle on the Cowskin. They were a general mixture of cattle which were close herded during the day and corralled at night. Cattle were not allowed to run loose in that neighborhood, as a very few of the cornfields were fenced.

I had only one desire at this time and that was to learn to ride, to shoot a pistol, and to throw a rope. I would practice all day long and by spring I was fairly good at all of them. Our saddle horses were of the small, mustang type, and I soon could ride the hardest bucking ones we had on the ranch, and liked it. I usually had from one to three broncos in my string to break. The smoking and drinking habits with which I hal left Ohio had by this time entirely

10

disappeared, and I never gave them a thought. I was interested solely in cattle and horses.

There was an abundance of game, prairie chickens, quail, jack rabbits, and some antelope. That fall I killed my first antelope and turkey with my Winchester rifle which my mother had sent on to me from home. This little rim-fire had its advantages, and I would not have traded it for any make of rifle that I knew of at that time. It was very short and light, and I could shoot it with accuracy by holding it free from the body with one hand, like shooting a pistol. I made a scabbard out of cowhide for it, and hung it from the horn of my saddle. The barrel went between the stirrup leathers; it was not noticeable because of its shortness, and it was not in the way of either roping or riding. I carried this little rifle with me for a good many years.

I learned a great deal during that year about cow camps and cow punchers from the ranch hands and cowboys that I met on Cowskin Creek. Among the men on the ranch that year was an old-timer named Frank Struthers, who had been an old Chisholm Trail driver, especially when Wichita was the end of the trail. He had been a companion and friend of the Clements brothers. They, together with a couple more of their kinsfolk who were a part of their gang, had killed nearly fifty men in gun fights. It was from Struthers that I learned the tricks of a quick draw—to take it easy and make the first shot count. Struthers had been a killer, but his nerves were now shot and he was a frightened wreck of a man.

In the spring the boss gave me a mustang; I bought a good double-cinch saddle, spurs, chaps, Coffeyville boots, big hat, and all the things that are necessary to make a real cow-puncher, including a .45 six-shooter. There had been more or less talk about the President of the United States' (Grover

Cleveland) ordering the cattle out of Oklahoma and throwing the territory open for settlement. In the early spring I bade the Cowskin Creek good-by, and left for the cow country. I do not believe I would have traded places with anyone I knew at that time.

In a couple of weeks I met the boss herder of the 4-D outfit, whose name was Ben Brice, at their camp on the Salt Fork of the Arkansas River. He was getting ready to trail two thousand head of cattle to the Brazos River country, in Texas, and he hired me. The outfit had about one hundred head of saddle horses, two wagons, about fifteen riders, a secretary, captain, cook, and helper. It does not require so many horses on a trail herd as it does on regular roundup work. These cattle were not being trailed to any market, but for the purpose of broadening them out and making them heavier for the market in the fall. We trailed them all summer in a circuitous route, avoiding all of the old trails from Texas to the Kansas markets. We kept on good grass as much as possible and near water, heading back toward a shipping point in the fall when, as finished beef, the herd would be ready for market.

At first I was not put on as a full cow hand, but rode all of the time, first at one position then another. I also helped the cook and the horse wrangler. Two mountain lions followed us and were seen almost every day either ahead of or behind the herd. They were treated as part of the outfit, and were never molested in any way. They stayed with us for at least a month.

A trail herd of this size would string out for a distance of about a mile and was about fifty yards wide. The distance covered in a day would be twelve or fourteen miles, varying according to the grass and water. The herd would be grazed along, beginning at daylight, and by the time the sun was from one to two hours high they all would be strung out, and moving along steadily. In a general way all cattle had their regular places in the herd on the trail. The same ones would be in the lead each day and the same ones would be behind. The timid ones would be on the outside of the bunch. The riders rode on each side of the herd, and the wagons usually brought up the rear.

The cattle were thrown off the trail about the middle of the afternoon, and grazed into camp for a couple of miles. At dark they were bunched, and the boys had regular shifts, standing guard during the night. The horses had a night and day herding, and it was the horse wrangler's job, when necessary, to help the cook. Part of my job was to gather a couple of sacks of buffalo chips each day, for firewood was very scarce. In fact, whenever we found any wood we hauled it with us. We passed near the Charles Goodnight ranch on the West Red River in Palo Duro Canyon, brand, "J. A."

I was considered a very good singer and often sang around the campfire. One of the favorite songs which had just come out was "Jessie James"; we sang it this way:

Jesse James was a lad that killed many a man,
He robbed the Danville train.
But that dirty little coward that shot Mr. Howard,
And laid poor Jesse in his grave.

Poor Jesse had a wife to mourn for his life,
Three children they were brave.
But that dirty little coward that shot Mr. Howard,
And laid poor Jesse in his grave.

Jesse was a man, a friend to the poor,
He never would cause any pain.

13

And with his brother Frank he robbed the
    Chicago bank
And stopped the Glendale train.

It was his brother Frank that robbed the
    Gallitan bank,
And carried the money from the town.
It was at this very place that they had a little race,
And they shot Captain Sheets to the ground.

It was on a Saturday night Jesse was home,
Talking with his family brave.
Robert Ford came along like a thief in the night,
And laid poor Jesse in his grave.

The people held their breath when they heard of
    Jesse's death,
And wondered how he came to die.
It was one of the gang called Little Robert Ford,
He shot poor Jesse on the sly.

It was on this trail that I saw my first man shot and killed. The herd was passing a few miles one side of a town in northern Texas, and one of the boys had been in town. On his return I saw him tell Brice something. After the cattle had been thrown off the trail to feed, Brice asked me if I would like to go to town with him. I felt very much elated to think that the boss would ask me to go with him. On our way there he told me that he might have some trouble in town, and asked me to stick around. We had just tied our horses to a hitching post, and turned toward a saloon, when we were met by a big burly Negro, part Indian. There wasn't a word spoken but they both pulled their guns.

Brice fired from the hip; the Negro's gun was not fired, and it fell with him to the ground. He was shot near the heart. I was standing only a few feet from Brice. My hand had gone unconsciously to the butt of my gun, but I did not draw.

Brice stepped back toward me and we stood close together. I was not frightened or excited but very much alert, watching for something to happen and fully intending to take an active part in it.

Several men came out of the saloon, and two of them approached us. After a few minutes talk, Brice handed one of them a ten dollar bill to cover the expense of burying the Negro, and we all went into the saloon where Brice set up the drinks for the house. We did a little shopping and rode back to camp. There was never anything further said about the matter that I know of.

CHAPTER THREE

TRAILING SOUTH

I SOON BECAME A FAVORITE with all the boys, and was nick-named "The Kid." I seemed to have the gift of remembering all the songs I heard from either the dance halls or the cow punchers. I sang such songs as "Sam Bass," "Tom Sherman's Barroom," "Zebra Dunn," "Chisholm Trail," and "Jack of Diamonds." Anyway the boys thought I could sing and liked to hear me, and from that time on I sang around many a fire on the cow camps throughout the West.

I was picked up one night by my friends while in a honky-tonk in a Texas town, and carried to the stage, where I sang a song called "Don't Send My Boy to Prison." At about the third encore a stagehand helped me pick up nearly a hatful of silver, mostly dollars. I was not quite fifteen years old and was nearly knocked down by the money. I returned to my friends in the audience and spent the entire contribution in buying drinks for the house; I drank lemonade. Later that same night I was placed on top of a table near the center of the beer hall, and sang "Tom Sherman's Barroom," which went as follows:

As I was passing Tom Sherman's Barroom,
Tom Sherman's barroom so early one morn.
There I spied a once handsome cowboy,
All dressed in white linen as tho for the grave.

Go beat your drum slowly and play your fife lowly,
Play the death march as I'm carried along.
Take me to the graveyard and throw the sod o'er me,
For I'm a poor cowboy and I know I've done wrong.

T'was once in my saddle I used to be dashing,
T'was once in the saddle I used to be gay
I first got to gambling from that got to drinking,
Got into this fuss and I'll go to my grave.

Go write a letter to my gray-haired mother,
And break the news to my sister so dear.
But there is another more dear than mother or sister,
I know she will weep when she learns I am here.

Go gather around you a crowd of gay cowboys,
And tell them the story of their comrade's sad fate.
Tell one and the other before they go farther,
To stop their wild ways before it's too late.

Get six jolly cowboys to carry my coffin,
Get six pretty maidens to bear up my pall.
Put bunches of roses all over my coffin,
Put roses to deaden the clods as they fall.

Go beat your drums slowly and play your fife lowly,
And play the death march as I'm carried along.
Take me to the graveyard and throw the sod o'er me,
For I'm a poor cowboy and I know I've done wrong.

The proprietor of the place offered me fifty dollars a night
to stay there and sing, but I left town the next day with my

companions and friends. I never sang for money, though many times afterward the above-mentioned scene was repeated.

Among the men who went out with that drive was Henry Starr. He had a strain of Indian blood in him, and was about two years older than I. From the start we became fast friends, and by the time we reached the Brazos River we were inseparable companions. Neither of us drank any liquor but I began to smoke cigarettes again. We were good riders, and were considered the best pistol shots in the outfit. I always kept the dogs of a six-shooter filed down until they were about a hair trigger. You cannot do good work with a hard-pulling gun. I was never very good at fanning,[1] but shot very well from the hip with either hand.

At this time a good many of the old buffalo hunters were still in the country. Some were freighters, farmers, or had small cow outfits; others were ranchers. Some went into the Indian Territory and became squaw men. A few, a rare few, joined in the outdoor sport of chasing outlaws, or broke into the profession themselves. Some became sheriffs.

The plains were strewn with buffalo bones, especially skulls, and nearly all of them had dry hides and curly wool on them. Quite often we found a stand where hunters had shot buffalo. On the ground scattered about would be many empty rifle shells.

Our trail herd was gathered and bunched west of the Arkansas River, and south of the Salt Fork of the Arkansas in the Indian Territory. We first trailed westerly, probably about 150 miles, then crossed the Cimarron River and trailed southwesterly between the Cimarron and the North

[1] A single-action pistol was shot rapidly by stripping back the hammer with left hand, while holding the trigger down with the right. This was called "fanning."

18

Canadian River. Then we turned west and followed the Canadian into the Panhandle of Texas. Then nearly south again, crossing many small streams on the way, still continuing in a southerly direction until we reached the Brazos River about 250 miles from where we had left the Canadian River.

We had been over four months on the trail. The cattle, having taken on weight, were now all in good condition, and the herd was ready to drive to some shipping point. Starr and I, together with two other boys, left the outfit at Big Spring to go to Mexico.

Sweetwater was a lively cowtown. It was here that Bat Masterson had killed a notorious character who had come into a dance hall where Bat was dancing with a girl, had shot and killed the girl and wounded Bat. Masterson shot from the floor and killed him. I got to know Bat quite well and saw him from time to time for several years. Bat was one of the men who had taken part in the Indian fight at Adobe Wells a few years before this.

In due time we fetched up at a crossing of the Pecos River, some fifty miles above its mouth. There was a settlers' store, post office, and saloon at the Vinegaroon water hole, west of the Pecos. I have forgotten the name of the fellow who ran the place, but he was the man who "made the law west of the Pecos."[2] A sign over his door read "The Jersey Lily."

With one pack horse we drifted up the Río Grande—the country of horned toads, diamondback rattlers, tarantulas, road runners, Gila monsters, and all the rest of the lizard family. It was said that the road runner killed the rattlesnake by laying a circle of prickly pears around him while he was asleep, then waking him up; he would become so angry that he would bite himself and die rather than cross

2 Judge Bean.

19

the circle of thorns. I never saw this happen but I have seen many small circles of the prickly pears in the semidesert country where the roadrunner lived, and have upon examination on several occasions found the bones of the snake inside the circle.

It was spring when we again crossed the Río Grande into Chihuahua, Mexico, having come down from the head of the Río Conchos to Presidio. It was a wonderful cow country where cattle are beef all the year round. During our stay in Chihuahua we took considerable part in the social functions, one of which I remember very well.

It was a fandango, or *baile* (Mexican dance). The trouble started this way. Across the room from where I was standing, near an opening in the wall, was a small side room where gambling was going on. Two of our boys were dancing and one was in the gambling room. I heard a crash and a shot, and a girl came stumbling through the door of the small room with a chair hanging around her neck. A Mexican followed through the door with blood running down from his neck over a white shirt. One of my companions was close behind him with a smoking pistol in his hand.

Everything was confusion and the two men behind the bar began to shoot. There didn't seem to be many guns among the dancers, although you were not asked to take off your guns when you danced. Everyone hit the floor except those who had hurried to the door. Only one light was burning. From my position I had seen every move that had been made.

I called to our boys to leave the hall without any further shooting. Most of the shooting had come from behind the bar. I started breaking a few bottles behind the bar over the heads of the barkeepers who stooped down out of sight and quit shooting.

20

My companions were by now just about out of the front door, although there was quite a jam there. Everybody seemed to want to get out at once. Two men on the floor were doing some shooting, and I tried to keep them quiet by scattering a little lead in their direction, also. I had backed up until I was in the window. It was not safe for me to try to get to the door. When I saw the last of our boys go out, I fell out backward as it was dangerous to turn my back. I left there as a rear guard for our party, with a gun in each hand in full action, holding back the mob of enraged Mexicans whose *señoritas* had shown marked preference for the light-haired gringos. I was gathered up by my comrades and, as our horses were near by, we soon left there.

CHAPTER FOUR

HENRY AND BELLE STARR

IN A FEW DAYS STARR AND I alone headed for the Pecos River country and the north. We crossed into New Mexico in quite a hurry, for we were not far ahead of some Texas Rangers who did not catch up with us because we had better horses. We were not afraid of them but did not court any trouble. The lower Pecos area was quite bushy, and a generally no-good country.

Starr's name was now being mentioned very often in connection with bank robberies. It seems as though he had been recognized by someone who knew him. He was raised in that country. I read a great deal, and got Starr started to reading. Our favorites at this time were *The Life and Tragic Death of Jesse James* and *The Younger Brothers*. James had been killed only a couple of years before, and he was still being talked about. From that time on I always owned the best horses that I could buy and often went far, solely for the purpose of getting a good thoroughbred horse. He is the horse that can travel long distances.

When we went up into the Pecos River country it was about three years after Billy the Kid was killed by Pat Garrett, who was still sheriff. The Kid seemed to have been a favorite among the natives; they liked him. Garrett was not especially well liked outside of his home town. He, too, was a killer.

Cattle rustling in the Kid's day was not considered much of a crime, and most of the cow outfits who lived in the big ranch houses carried along branding irons themselves. I heard two or three accounts about how Billy the Kid was killed. One of them claimed that it was not the Kid that Garrett killed, but from the account I was given at Fort Sumner I do not think there was ever any doubt but that Garrett killed the Kid in the Maxwell home. The same version was told at the Chisum ranch by several of the cowboys who knew the Kid well.

John Chisum, the owner of the ranch, was dead at this time, and the ranch was being run by his brother. I worked for a short time for the Chisum outfit, which went by the name of "The Long Rail" or "Jingle Bob."

The real story as I got it was to the effect that shortly before the Kid was killed, he had made a spectacular escape from the jail at Lincoln, over the top of Murphy's store, killing two men in doing so, and was spending the night at Fort Sumner with a lady friend. They wanted a bucket of water or something to eat, and the Kid went to the Maxwell house, which was just a short distance away, to get it. Garrett by mere chance was in the house, talking to Maxwell; there were no lights in the house when the Kid walked in, but he saw there was someone in the room, though he could not make out who it was.

"Quien es?" he called out to Maxwell, meaning "Who it it?"

Maxwell was in bed and Garrett shot in the dark without speaking, killing the Kid. The Kid did not shoot.

I created a bit of a flurry at Fort Sumner, because, so they said, my face and general appearance bore such a marked resemblance to Billy the Kid. I could have won a home there among the *señoritas* without very much trouble as Billy had been a great favorite. Lincoln had been a bad town for killings but had now quieted down, since nearly all the bad men on both sides of the Lincoln County War had been killed.

On our way east we spent several days in Wagon Mound, with its natural meadows, big cottonwood trees, and plenty of spring water. I did not like to leave there. The girls had just the right amount of Mexican in them to make them attractive. I fully expected to return there and make a permanent camp but never did. However, I have always thought of it with pleasant memories, as the camp between the little capped buttes at the head of the coulee.

In leaving that section of the country we went via the old Cimarron Cutoff of the Santa Fe Trail to Cimarron Crossing on the Arkansas River, in Kansas, just a few miles west of Dodge City. We camped for quite a spell on the Arkansas at Pawnee Rock, and then we drifted back into the Indian Territory.

We saw a good many of the famous Western characters in Hays, and Dodge City, Kansas, but never knew any of them very well. We did not stay in towns any more than we could help, and never loafed very long in the saloons or dance halls where they spent most of their time. We were not much more than boys in looks and very little attention was paid to us. Henry Starr and I were companions for three or four years, during which time we worked for many outfits in the southwest and rode over all that country together. We knew a great many of the ranchers on Red River, and far out on the Canadian, Cimarron, and Arkansas rivers. Most of their brands were characters, such as a pitchfork,

24

jug, frying pan, horseshoe, bow and arrow, trey of diamonds, ace of clubs, and 666. Not so many letters were used as now.

At that time there was a strip of land lying between Kansas and Texas (now the northwestern part of Oklahoma), which was known as "No Man's Land," and it was quite a hangout for outlaws. Only United States marshals and their deputies could make arrests in "No Man's Land." This strip of the country lay due north of the Texas Panhandle; the North Canadian River lay nearly in the center, and the Cimarron, on the northern edge; there was plenty of grass and water. Nearly all the creeks had cottonwood and box elders on them. Anderson Creek was rough and rocky. North and South Moccasin, Cold Water, and Gulf creeks were all favorite hide-outs.

Starr and I covered a very wide range for saddle-horse days. We were well acquainted with the Big Bend country of the Río Grande, and at one time we crossed the Colorado River at Lees Ferry, just above the Grand Canyon, Arizona. We spent a good deal of time in Indian camps, learning to tan buckskin, and to know a good deal about Indians and their ways. I became good at talking the Indian sign language, and have had some good Indian friends.

Chief Big Bear Pontiac, who in later years became associated with General Motors, and is famous through the Pontiac cars, was a good friend. Big Bear went with the first shipment of Pontiac automobiles to Australia. He traveled a great deal over Europe and South America. He was at that time a wonderful singer. He was a real entertainer, and I never tired of listening to him tell stories or sing. We were friends for many years in Montana.

Here is a little story that illustrates home life in an Indian camp. One day I came to an Indian camp at the west end of the Sweetgrass Hills in northern Montana. It was the

25

home of Chief Big Bear's father, mother, and other relatives. The Chief was a young man then. The Indians were all rejoicing and feeling very happy. About a year before the children had brought home a young sand-hill crane which they had found and raised as a pet. All summer long they caught him fish and frogs. They named him "Dick." He grew fast and by early fall was about full sized. He slept in the tipi because he was very much afraid of coyotes. Big Bear told me what had happened.

Mama used to go out on the prairie with Dick and pitch him up in the air and talk to him. "Dick you must learn to fly. You must get your wings strong." Dick soon began to fly short distances around the camp. When ducks and geese began to fly south Dick would walk around among the children and look at the sky and cry.

One day when the wind was blowing from the north and ducks and geese were flying south Mama said, "Dick now it's time you were going south. It will be too cold for you to stay here this winter. The creeks and ponds will all freeze over and we can't get you any fish or frogs and you will freeze. So come now and we will see if you are ready to go."

Mama sewed a piece of red flannel around Dick's leg and we all went out to see him off. He seemed to know all about it and understood. We went to a little knoll and formed a circle. Dick would hop up from the ground and flop his wings then walk around to each one of us and cry. Mama would keep on telling him to make up his mind but Dick would only cry. All at once Dick quit crying and stood very still. He walked to about the middle of the ring, began to flop his wings, jumped up a couple of times and took off. Looking into the sky we couldn't see or hear anything.

26

Dick circled around us crying all the time going higher and higher. About the time we couldn't hear Dick cry any more we heard the peculiar croaking noise of the sand-hill crane and could see a large flock very high up, almost out of sight. It looked as though Dick had joined the flock and was gone.

On the early morning of my arrival at the Indian camp the Indian had heard a commotion outside the tipi, dogs barking and making a fuss. On going out, there stood Dick showing unmistakable signs that he was glad to be back home. The red flannel was still sewed around his leg.

Henry Starr and I built a small cabin in the Cookson Hills located in the northeastern part of the Indian Nation, where we spent considerable time. The mountains were well timbered and it was difficult to get anyone out of them once he hid there. These mountains made a great rendezvous for bandits and getaway men. Later that same summer we built another small cabin in the Wichita Mountains in the southwest corner of the Indian Nation. These mountains provided a paradise for game of every description, such as all kinds of deer, antelope, wild turkey, etc. They were well timbered, watered, and had an abundance of grass.

Nearly all the horses in that country were of the mustang type, so a man on a 950-pound near-thoroughbred was in very little danger of being caught up with. There were almost no telegraph or telephone wires in that section in those days, and a posse could not head a man off if his getaway route was well laid out. There were a great many robberies and killings going on. Oklahoma, Kansas, and the section were full of officers of the law. It is my opinion, however, that a very small percentage of the bank robbers and bandits were ever apprehended.

27

The James gang had put the fear of God into so many of the bank employees that there was not very much resistance offered. Those pioneer robbers had made bank-robbing easy for the other fellows. Sometimes the robbers would be out of town before the citizens knew what had happened, and often not a shot was fired.

I met Belle Starr for the first time in Tomilson's Hall. It was a dance hall in Laredo, Texas. She was a slim-waisted brunette, with a trim ankle, and as a dance-hall girl, good to look at. She sang and danced well. She was not working regularly in Tomilson's Hall, although she took some part in dancing on the floor and sang now and then from the platform. She had been married years prior to my meeting her to a man by the name of Sam Starr, a half-blood Indian. They took up land on the Canadian and started a ranch there. Sam was a horse thief and was killed a few years later. I never knew whether or not Henry Starr and Sam were related. Henry had some Indian blood in him, but he didn't resemble a half-blood. I understood Belle was a friend of the James and Younger brothers and that they had been welcome visitors at Belle's Canadian River ranch.

Laredo was a real woolly cow town in those days. It was mostly adobe buildings with some wooden ones here and there. Nuevo Laredo was across the Río Grande and was quite a town also. Tomilson's Hall was very much like the general run of beer and dance halls all over the west. It consisted of a room about thirty or forty feet wide, and about sixty or more feet long. At the end opposite the entrance there was a raised platform with a piano on it used for vaudeville stunts, usually song and dance artists. A long bar ran the length of one side of the room, leaving a considerable space clear for dancing. Girls walked around among the tables, sitting down with the men to talk and drink between the dances. After the dance you were supposed to escort your partner to the bar and buy drinks. She received checks which she later cashed as commissions on the drinks that had been sold to her partners for the evening. There was no admission charged for the show, and quite often there would be gambling games going on in a corner of the hall, or a small back room, to further entertain the casual visitor.

I believe Belle Starr had a real affection for Henry Starr, disregarding the big sums of money which he sometimes had. He was a liberal spender when it came to buying nice things for Belle. I do not know whether she and Henry were ever married. After our visit to Laredo, Starr and I left together. We were joined about the middle of the afternoon by Belle. We carried two pack horses and each one of us had our own bedroll. Belle wore men's clothing, and with her hair done up under her hat it was difficult to tell her from a man. She made a fine-looking cowpuncher, and despite the fact that she was fifteen years older than I was, she had all the appearance of a young woman.

She was of a happy-go-lucky disposition—met you always with a smile and had a ready laugh. She never complained about the hardships of a pack outfit, and they were many, for at that time a great portion of the southern part of Texas was hard to get through even with a pack horse. There was very little prairie land. Most of the country was covered with mesquite brush or juniper cedar.

There were many women on the southwest frontier who used names other than their own, and frequently one would let it be known on the quiet that she was Belle Starr. The Belle Starr of whom I just spoke was known simply as "Belle" to her associates in the dance halls, and was known only to her intimate friends as "Belle Starr." It was a difficult matter for any tinhorn gambler or Chesterfieldian frontiersmen to make love to Belle as she was too handy with a six gun.

It was generally understood that Belle was the leader of a band of bank robbers or all round bad men. I am not saying this was not true during some portion of her career, as she had been very active for a good many years before my time. I wouldn't be surprised that if during the time I have just mentioned Belle was not laying low. I have heard her tell of some of the parts she played in holdups of earlier days.

There was a territory some fifty or seventy-five miles west of Austin which was almost impossible to get through. It was solid scrub timber, mostly juniper, mesquite, and rocks. After reaching the Colorado River north of Austin our trip was more pleasant. We went up the Colorado River northwesterly nearly to Sweetwater, then northeasterly, keeping most of the time in the broad-blade grass country.

It was no trouble to keep your movements hidden from sheriffs or posses if you desired, and no trouble to get meat. Game was plentiful. Nearly all the ridges were covered with oak timber, not too thick to interfere with travel.

There was plenty of water, grass, and wood. Very little of the country was fenced. If you wanted to go through a fence without leaving any sign, it was an easy matter to pull up two or three fence posts, lay them down, cross over them, and set the posts back. I have heard or read many stories about posses chasing bandits out West. However, I never knew a posse to follow bandits very far into timbered country.

I always thought that all of eastern Oklahoma and a wide strip of Texas running northeast and southwest through the entire state, just a little east of center, was made to order for bandits in which to get away from the sheriffs. I personally knew several men of that class, and they felt perfectly safe at all times there. It was when they would go to town, get full of liquor, and do too much talking that they got killed or picked up.

It was necessary to find a regular ford or crossing on only a few of the rivers in that country, although there was considerable quicksand and in some places adobe mud, which was bad. What you wanted to look our for was not to get up against a bank on the other side. It was not much trouble to push a horse down a bank to get him into the water. Just tie something over his eyes, turn him around a couple of times, then walk him over.

We journeyed by easy stages on a circuitous route for over a month. We spent very few nights in the towns or in hotels, usually lying out some distance from the main trails. We separated in the northeastern part of the Indian Territory—Belle leaving for her ranch on the Canadian, and Henry and I going toward the Cookson Hills. About a year and a half later I last saw Belle at her ranch on the Canadian.

31

CHAPTER FIVE

I TAKE A RIDE IN THE APPALACHIANS

THAT FALL I WAS TAKEN SICK with typhoid fever, and was taken by my companions to Wichita, Kansas. After I recovered I again spent the balance of the winter on the Cowskin Creek at the ranch of Mr. Eberly. I felt very much at home there. In the feeding corrals we had at this time about 650 beeves, and 1200 to 1500 hogs, all on full feed. We bought thousands of bushels of shelled corn and many tons of roughness hay. Corn, as I remember, was eighteen cents a bushel; I mean shelled corn. Mr. Eberly left me in charge of the ranch during his absence on occasional business trips, providing a book of signed checks for me to use in the purchase of hay and grain.

This was during the winter of the big blizzard. For three days the temperature stood around 26° below zero, with a terrific gale blowing, and plenty of snow. All kinds of livestock and game were frozen to death—cattle, antelope, jack rabbits, quail, and prairie chickens. I found whole coveys of quail sitting in the grass frozen, and some on the snow with their wings spread out as though they had frozen while in the air.

I did chores and general work around the ranch. Among other things I had to look after nine head of skim-milk calves. When the storm first struck I tried to drive them into the woodshed, which was built up against the dwelling house, but succeeded in getting only seven of them in. Two missed the opening, and I couldn't get them back. When the storm was over I found them just around the corner of the shed, frozen stiff. Fat hogs climbed one upon the other under the roughness feeder and smothered to death. I hauled many a four-horse load of them to the soap factory in Wichita where they were sold for one cent a pound.

Mrs. Eberly had just purchased a dozen Buff Cochin chickens and had a good cornstalk house built for them; they were all frozen to death and fell from the roost to the ground. I remember having seen the turkeys fill up with grain at one of the big piles of shelled corn which were on the ground and then fly to the top of some big black-walnut trees just before the blizzard struck. When the storm was over they all flew back unharmed.

During the height of the storm, in order to get water from the well, we would tie a small rope around a big Norwegian named Adam Reeder, and send him out to the bucket-and-chain type of well, and then haul him back again. No one went to the barn during the storm; but the horses were all right when we got to them, though very hungry. They had chewed big notches in their mangers.

After the storm was over a little band of men of the neighborhood got together and went out to the westward to look for a man and daughter named Cook. They had gone to make proof on his land claim. I went along with the searching party, and on the road we found a man, sitting on his wagon seat, frozen stiff and dead. There was a ball of ice about the size of a baseball on each cheek; both horses were

33

frozen to death in their harness. We met Cook and his daughter coming back; they had not left their sod house during the storm and had fared pretty well though they had burned all the woodwork in the house.

I made a trip back to Ohio that spring. I was nineteen years old. During this absence from the West my friend Henry Starr was sent to the penitentiary in Arkansas. Later (1915), I understood he held up two banks at once in Stroud, Oklahoma, and was shot from his horse. I never saw him again, although he was in evidence throughout the West for many years after.

Ohio did not seem the same to me as it had when I left there. Most of my companions had gone from bad to worse; some of them were serving time for various crimes. The few left were hard drinkers, and seemed very narrow. The place did not appeal to me, so my stay was short.

Major Weiler, of Johnson City, Tennessee, owned a very fine Appaloosa mare in Ohio which he wanted shipped to his home. The rail route going south was a very roundabout one, and the freight rates were very high, so I agreed to ride her through the country.

I was equipped with the same outfit that I had brought from the West, and attracted a lot of attention on the trip. I had a six-shooter, .44 cailber rifle, spurs, my big hat, and all the other apparel of the Far West. In all the towns through which I passed, I was asked many questions, and my arrival in each was as though some noted stranger had come in.

I crossed the Ohio River at Ironton, then turned up the river to Catlettsburg, Kentucky, at the mouth of the Big Sandy River. About the middle of the afternoon, just after leaving Catlettsburg, I passed a drove of cattle coming into town from up the Big Sandy. I was eyed very closely by a very tall man with a big hat, riding a good mule. He was in charge of the cattle. The next evening, just before sundown, I was overtaken by this same man; his mule was lathered with perspiration. I was averaging about fifty miles a day so he must have ridden his mule pretty hard to catch up with me. He told me later that he had wound up his business in Catlettsburg as quickly as he could in order to overtake me and had ridden almost all night and day. He was very curious about me; he said that all of the strangers coming into that country were looked upon with suspicion. He asked me a great many questions. I must have satisfied him although he expressed anxiety about my welfare, and did not want to see me go on up the river.

By this time we had reached the neighborhood of Paintsville, Kentucky, and we spent the night together in a small cabin on the side of the mountain. In it there were two big boys, a couple of girls, and an older woman; they all chewed tobacco.

I gave them all that I had in my pocket. It was fine cut. That night they all got fairly drunk on peach brandy and corn whisky. I did not like the trend of their conversation as they talked too much about my horse and my outfit. I was not at all afraid of them but did not care to have any trouble. I became somewhat uneasy about my horse and spent the night in the small log barn with her. However my fears were without foundation, and in the morning, when they had sobered somewhat, we all had a fine breakfast of brook trout, wild turkey, and corn bread.

I had been warned several times, while coming up the river, about the danger of trying to go through that country, because of the Hatfield and McCoy feud, which was at its height at that time. As I had never heard of it, I had no uneasiness about it, and continued on my way. I was also told it was always open season on revenue men in that section.

The man with the good mule and I rode together until late that afternoon, when we reached the neighborhood of Pikeville. We had become well acquainted with each other, and he tried very hard to persuade me to go home with him, and to go through by way of Big Stone Gap, but I had planned my route by the way of Lebanon, Virginia, and would not change my plans. We separated at the river forks. I had with me a road map which had been used by Major Weiler during the War of the Rebellion, which showed all the roads and trails through these mountains, and it proved very useful. I was making good time and had no delays, yet in some mysterious way, my coming was known ahead of me all the way up the river. In all the small towns I passed through—Christiansburg, Paintsville, Pikeville, and others—I was put through a lot of questioning and conversation. The citizens up that way were just naturally curious.

Just before dark one evening, I was stopped in the road by two men who told me to go with them. I finally consented, and one of them walked ahead of me and the other behind. They were rough-looking characters, with big-rimmed black hats and bad-looking eyes. Each had a long-barreled squirrel rifle. They did not take my gun or pistol away from me, and it would have been a simple matter to have shot both of them had it become necessary to do so. We fetched up at a small cabin where there was a sharp bend in the creek and road. There was a family living in the cabin. They unsaddled my horse and took the saddle, bridle, guns, and all into a side room, and turned the horse loose in a small pasture.

During supper they asked me a multitude of questions. Shortly afterwards two more men arrived and we sat up till late into the night while I told them a great deal about the West, the cattlemen and gunmen, cowpunchers and bank robbers. They made one of the most interested audiences I ever talked to.

36

The next morning the Western conversation was all gone over again. Other neighbors arrived, and during the day I had to give them an exhibition of pistol-shooting. When I left that evening I was a friend of them all, and I believe it was with sincere regret that they saw me go away. I fully expected to meet some of them someday in the West, but I never did. There were no introductions so I don't know whether they were Hatfields or McCoys.

It was nearly dark when I finally left my new friends and started over Scaggs Mountain for Virginia. The road was little more than a trail, switching back and up the mountain side and through very heavy timber which made it very dark, so dark that I gave the mare her head. I couldn't see anything. At the foot of the mountain on the Virginia side, I came upon a roaring torrent. I got off the horse, lit some matches, and saw that the road went into it, so got back on my horse and took a chance. The stream was swift and yellow with mud. The water ran just over my saddle. On the other side I came out of the river into a heavy forest on a flat bottom. About a mile or two farther on I heard a dog bark to my left and my horse stopped in a footpath which lead to a low rail fence. We hopped over this and found ourselves in a small clearing with a cabin where, after a good deal of argument with a man, I was permitted to spend the night. As I remember, one of his objections was that there was a cow in the pasture with a broken shoulder and that my horse might do her further damage. I told him that if we found the cow had been hurt by the horse that I would pay him the price of her in the morning.

Two grown girls and the man were the only occupants of the cabin, and one of the girls held the lightwood torch while I ate corn pone and drank a gourdful of milk, all of which was served on a puncheon table, which stood on a puncheon floor. After talking a long time, I was quite ready to go to bed, and the old man pointed to a very high bed shoved against the wall in a corner of the same room. It may seem strange but I was always very bashful when in the presence of women, so there was a good deal of stalling around on my part, before I could get my clothes off and get into bed. The girl then pitched the torch into the fireplace, which brightened up the fire, and both of them got into bed with me. Truth is stranger than fiction; I was scared of those girls; they did a lot of giggling, but I was too frightened to giggle, and got my face close to the wall and remained in that position until daylight.

The country along the Big Sandy River was very rough and rocky. The natives lived on the mountain sides in poorly built cabins with mud and stick chimneys. In front were old, broken-down rail fences overgrown with briers and weeds. If the cabin was so situated as to command a view of the road for some distance, the approaching stranger would be met by children of all ages, lined up on the fence, and with the invariable greeting:

"Howdy stranger, give me a chaw of tobacker, if you chaw. I don't know if you chaw or not. Do you chaw?"

The last night before reaching Johnson City, I spent in a small town named, I think, Unionville. Back of the barn at the place where I spent the night there was a pond, and a dock, built just a few inches above the water, which ran out into deep water and was used for washing horses. I had never heard of anything like it before. I had the mare washed so she was very clean and pretty when we got into Johnson City the next day. It was the fifteenth day after leaving northern Ohio. The mare was in splendid shape—much better in fact, than when we started on the journey.

I remained in eastern Tennessee for several months.

While there I became well acquained with Governor Bob Taylor and his family, Alf and Nat Taylor, who lived, I believe, at Elizabethtown. I attended a few dances where Bob Taylor did part of the fiddling. Here is a story I heard Alf Taylor tell on several occasions: About 1867 the government sent a peace committee out to Medicine Creek, Kansas, to make a treaty with the Plains Indians, who had been on the warpath for some time. There were several thousand Indians gathered for the medicine talk. The government party was mostly army officers and a few newspaper reporters; Alf was with them.

It seems that a half-blood Indian who talked English was thrown off his horse. He was trying to get back on but the horse was afraid of him. The man kept cussing and kicking the horse until he saw he was not getting anywhere so he tried a different tack. He slowly eased up the hackamore rope until he could touch the horse on the neck where he stroked him very softly and slowly and kept repeating in a very soft voice, "You nice, big mean son of a b——. You big, fine rotten son of a b——." A young Indian chief who couldn't speak English stood near by watching. After the man had gone the Indian chief walked over to one of the high army officers who was sitting down; he put his hand on the officer's shoulder and gently stroking him said, "You nice, big, fine, rotten son of a b——." The chief thought he was saying something nice to the officer. There was a near riot until the interpreter straightened the matter out.

I met Frank Stratton and General Wilder who were building the Cloudland Hotel on Roan Mountain, and made many trips up there with them. I also met Henry Ray, the sheriff of Watauga County. Henry was the kind of sheriff that everyone likes. He was a fine fellow and my ideal of a gentleman. I rode through the mountain country a good deal with him,

39

visiting many a still where we drank moonshine (corn whisky) and kissed all the babies. I never knew of Henry's arresting anybody for making whisky.

I soon tired of Johnson City, but during my stay there I spent a good deal of time around the office of the E. T. V. & G. railroad, brushing up on my telegraphy and practicing the getting on and off of moving trains. By the time I left I was fairly good as an operator. This stood me in good stead later on out West, where I worked as an operator three times on railroads. The practice of bumming my way in a country where I was not known rather appealed to me. I did not like to pay railroad fares, and as night was usually the best time for one to bum his way over the country, I spent very few nights in hotels.

Before leaving Tennessee I shipped my saddle, bridle, chaps, spurs, and all the rest of my cowboy outfit to Coffeyville, Kansas, and there my hoboing ended.

CHAPTER SIX

I TEAM UP WITH BLACK JACK

AFTER BUYING A GOOD SADDLE HORSE, and a lead horse for a light pack, I headed southwest, and visited Belle Starr's ranch on the Canadian River. The ranch was forty or fifty miles west of what is now Oklahoma City. Belle was at home, and there I met Charley Hardesty and the two Reed boys, Chub and George, from Missouri. Their father had served, so I was told, with Quantrell.

Speaking of Quantrell reminds me of an old man I met several years later in Montana; his name was John Bird, and he, too, had served with Quantrell. He lived in York which was in Trout Creek Gulch, Lewis and Clark County, Montana. He was somewhat stove up in the legs but his mind was as clear as a bell. Many were the stories he told me of the happenings during his days with the Quantrell outfit, and of his experiences while an associate of the James boys and the Younger brothers. It still was an amusing thought to him, what a good mark a bluecoat made to shoot at.

While at Belle's ranch I learned the "Bucking Bronco," a song which she was supposed to have composed:

My love is a cowboy. Wild bronchos he breaks,
But he's given up riding all for my sake.
One foot in the stirrup, a hand on the horn,
With a whoop and a yell he is mounted and gone.

The first time I met him, 'twas early one spring,
Riding a bronco, a high-headed thing.
He tipped me a wink as he gayly did go,
For he wished me to look at his bucking bronco.

The next time I saw him 'twas late in the fall,
A swinging the girls in Tomilson's Hall.
We laughed and we talked and we danced to and fro,
He promised he'd ne'er ride another bronco.

Now, all you young maidens, where'er you reside,
Beware of the cowboy who swings the rawhide.
He'll court you and pet you and leave you to go,
In the spring up the trail on his bucking bronco.

There were several more verses, but they were a little too racy to quote.

Belle's ranch did not differ very much from other well-to-do ranches in either Kansas or Oklahoma. The main building was made of logs, and the outbuildings were partly of logs and sod. She employed two men to plow and plant; and there was a good corral, and a fenced pasture. The living room, or main room of the ranch house, was about sixteen by twenty feet, furnished with up-to-date furniture, including a piano. I believe it was Belle's intention to build up an honest-to-goodness ranch, as she was an enthusiastic fancier of purebred stock, both cattle and horses.

After leaving her ranch I never went back into that section of the country for I heard about a year later that she had been shot and killed. Another reason I cared neither

42

to remain or return was that there were literally thousands of people from Kansas and other places pouring into that country. There seemed to be a regular stampede; a sod house appeared to be going up on every quarter section of land, and about every ten miles a town had been laid out. All of this didn't look good to me, and I was anxious to get away. Too much settlement for me.

The Miller family lived on the Cherokee strip, owning the famous "One Hundred and One" branding iron, and were beginning to grow cattle. From there I went west to the Purgatoire country, in southern Colorado, passing through the strip called "No Man's Land," crossing the Cimarron Cutoff trail at the Cimarron River Crossing, and came onto the Purgatoire River about halfway between Trinidad and Las Animas. These towns, together with Raton, New Mexico, which was on the south side of the range, were all very lively places, and still had some of the life of the old West left in them. The principal road through this section was the Santa Fe Trail.

If the section was noted for anything in particular, it was for its rough, tough bunch of men. It was also a hunter's paradise. All the deer family was represented as well as antelope, bear, mountain lions, and wolves in abundance. It was never any trouble to get meat, and was an ideal place to hold and fatten a bunch of beef in the summertime. Settlers and small ranchers were far apart. A great deal of the country, especially the benchland, was covered with juniper and pinion-pine timber.

Here I became acquainted with a character by the name of Black Jack Ketchum. His appearance indicated that there might be considerable Indian blood in him. Later his principal business, aside from hunting, was robbing trains and holding up banks. He was an expert with a rope and, whenever he saw a wolf, he could not resist the temptation to give chase either to rope or to shoot it. He was not, however, the man-killer type, and did not like to kill anyone. Black Jack's cabin, located on the middle fork of Purgatoire River in Colorado, was quite a hide-out for his friends and associates.

We left together and went over to the Pecos River country and on to the westward, visiting the old town of Taos, a little adobe settlement, going via the old town of Cimarron and through the Cimarron Canyon and Ute Park. Most of the summer was spent in and around Taos, Santa Fe, and Las Vegas. There were a few ranches or cow outfits there and we were welcome at all of them.

The burro and prospector played a very important part in the settling of the West. You could find the one's trails and the remains of the other's cabins in almost every gulch. The price of silver had gone down so low that it did not pay to work the mines. A few high-graders were all that remained in the old camps. Fort Union in the Turkey Mountains was in evidence. Wagon Mound was a good campground. It had big springs, natural meadows, and plenty of cottonwood trees.

That fall we worked on the C—— outfit in Arizona and spring found us with the Hash Knife outfit, in the Navajo country, of which Burton Mossman was manager for the Aztec Cattle Company. When we left the Hash Knife outfit the boys pitched a party in a barroom of Holbrook, and sat me up on the bar to sing some of my songs. All during this time I was known simply as the "Texas Kid"; no other name was either known or used.

Drifting north again, we spent considerable time in prospecting on and around Lava Plains, on the Broken Lava Plateau, in the Snake River country of southern Idaho. It was a wonderful place for hide-outs, for very few people except Indians ever went into that section. It was an interesting country too, because in spots there were cold springs, pools of water, and good grass. Turning east from southern Idaho, we headed for Jackson Hole, Wyoming.

One day we were overtaken by a boy, at the mouth of a short, steep gulch which came in from the north side of Trail Creek, in the Teton Mountains. He was not over fifteen or sixteen years old and was carrying the mail into the Hole on its first trip that spring. There was still considerable snow in the gulches, and it was just about as early as it was possible to take a horse over the trail from the post office at Marysvale. At the top of the gulch he had spied a big bear, walking along on a ledge of rocks, about a thousand feet above us. Looking up, I estimated the distance from us to be about a quarter of a mile. The boy was quite excited, and said his mother wanted him to get some bear oil for her. He pulled an old buffalo gun from under his leg and fired without getting off his horse. The bear slowly turned halfway around and fell dead. Of all the "pop shots" I have ever seen, that was the "popest." I helped the boy get the bear down the gulch. It had been shot through the brain.

Jackson Hole now became our permanent quarters; we made trips from time to time into Montana and other places. The Hole had become quite a rendezvous for long riders, bank robbers, and all kinds of bad men.

45

PART II

At Home in Jackson Hole, 1888–95

CHAPTER SEVEN

LIFE IN THE HOLE

JACKSON HOLE LIES DIRECTLY SOUTH of Yellowstone National Park in Wyoming; it is about twenty-five miles in length from north to south, and from two to several miles in width. Snake River runs south through it just a little west of the center, and flows out through a very mountainous and rocky canyon at the south end. As far as I knew at that time no one had ever gone through this canyon; the story was that even logs would be broken all to pieces making the trip.

The Grand Teton Mountains, rising to an altitude of about thirteen thousand feet, bound the Hole on the west; and from between two peaks of the Tetons the melting snow provides an ever-flowing stream of water which turns into a waterfall, with a sheer drop of several thousand feet. The water never reaches the bottom as it is carried away as spray and mist. As long as the sun shines there is a perpetual rainbow; and as a result of the scattered spray, there is a wonderful growth of ferns and timber. Under the Tetons on the benchlands between the mountains and Snake River are

49

Jackson Lake, Leigh Lake, Whitefish Lake, and Jenny Lake, along with other smaller ones.

There was a good deal of timber on the western side, and at irregular intervals, scattered through the Hole, were short butte-like ridges ranging in height from a few hundred to nearly a thousand feet, and from a quarter to about a mile long. At the southern end there were natural meadows which furnished the settlers with slough-grass hay. The Buffalo Fork of the Snake River came into the Hole at the north end, and the Gros Ventre River entered it a little south of the center from the east.

On the east side there were several trails coming into the Hole, and there was one at the south end of the Grand Tetons, on the west side over twelve thousand feet high. Another trail led in through the southwest corner of the Yellowstone Park via Lost River which ran underground. One ran up the Gros Ventre River, on the east side, going over to Green River. Chipmunk Pass, a trail very seldom used or known, went out from the southeasterly portion of the Hole. It was a very difficult trail to get over, and was used principally by those who had reasons to leave the Hole without the fact's being known.

Some years before my time some prospectors had brought a ditch from what was called "Ditch Creek," around the foothills for probably a mile and a half to Antelope Springs. The object was to work placer ground for gold. I never could find any gold worth while working in there. The gold on Snake River was so flaky and light, it was called "flour gold," and was very difficult to save although there seemed to be quite a lot of it.

When I first went into the Jackson Hole country, there was a settlement of Mormons in the lower end of the Hole, and a couple of squaw men on the Gros Ventre River. Near

50

Buffalo Fork of Snake River, which was near the south boundary of Yellowstone National Park, there lived a family by the name of Cunningham. A man from New York, named Ray Hamilton, who we understood was an actor, built a very fine cabin on Jackson Lake. He afterward drowned while crossing Buffalo Fork with an antelope on his saddle horse. There was some investigation about his death made from New York. There is no question in my mind but that he was drowned while crossing the river as stated above. The post office was called Marysvale.

I had built a cabin in Jackson Hole and called that my home. My first place was half-cabin, half dug-out and was located on Crystal Creek up the Gros Ventre River some miles from the Hole. A few years later I built a better one at Antelope Springs, in the Hole proper. During these years in Jackson Hole, I was always looking for a location for a ranch. No location less than one hundred miles from a settlement was considered. What correspondence I carried on was by various names. For several years I never wrote home. My companions were a homeless, reckless, straight-shooting, and hard-drinking set.

While in the Jackson Hole country I wore buckskin shirts, decorated with bear claws and trimmed with beaver. I had other clothes for the outside. I never had any pictures taken until after I became a rancher in Montana. As far as I know there was only one man in the entire wild bunch who ever knew my real name. I will call him "Skeeter." Skeeter spent some time with me later on the Montana ranch.

I believe I took the first wagon into Jackson Hole on its own wheels. There had been one packed in on horses prior to that time. Going down the Tetons, on the Hole side, I had a tree, top and all, tied to the hind axle for an additional rough lock, with a man riding in the treetop. It was

51

a three-reach spring wagon. I sat in the bottom, my back against the stationary seat, and a foot in each corner of the wagon box, well braced. At about the worst place there was, the rope which held the tree broke and I jumped clear of the outfit just as the wagon was going over endways. The tongue broke off short and stuck in the ground. We fetched up with the wagon upside down, on top of three horses. It was some mix-up. Later, the same wagon rolled down the mountain side near the south boundary of the Yellowstone Park and was never recovered.

If you were going to winter in the Hole it was necessary to kill your meat before the trails were blocked by deep snow. The elk and antelope would nearly all be gone by early winter. They went to the Red Desert which lay to the southeastward.

Fresh meat would keep all winter long either hung up with the hide on or thrown down into a snowdrift. However, we always jerked some meat and fish, which could be eaten without cooking, and was handy to carry on long trips. Our cooking grease was about half bear oil and half elk tallow. The Mormons always raised good gardens of rutabagas in the lower end of the Hole. They are very tender, crisp, and sweet. Because the ground froze or frosted nearly every month in the year, they could not raise a big variety of vegetables.

In the summer and fall the Hole was a paradise for game. The surrounding hills were full of elk, some moose, black-and whitetail deer, mountain lions, bear, antelope, coyotes, foxes, and many other fur-bearing animals. I have caught speckled trout in Crystal Creek (a clear-water creek which empties into the Gros Ventre River some twenty miles east of the Hole), that weighed eight pounds. I have counted during a ten-mile ride between Antelope Springs and the post office as many as two thousand antelope. A great many elk passed through the Hole in the fall of the year on the way to their winter range on the Red Desert. Occasionally some of them would stay in the Hole and become a menace to the settler's haystacks during the winter.

I lived and trapped one winter in a warm-spring district of the Hole which was a series of beaver meadows. A beaver meadow is what was once a beaver pond after the beavers have all been killed. The creek cuts a trench through the dam and drains the water out, usually leaving a level spot of land of one to three acres covered with good grass—ofttimes good enough to cut for hay. Two old bull elk, which had been whipped out of the herd by the younger bulls, became snowbound there and spent the winter with me. That is, we were camped close to each other.

The water never froze in the narrow channels that wound around through the marsh, but the snow was six or seven feet deep. The bulls would wade into the water to eat the slough grass and moss along the water's edge, underneath the snowbank. Sunshiny days they would leap out of the water, landing on their sides on the snow, and lie there until nearly evening, then slide back into the water. I moved about on a homemade pair of bear-paw snowshoes, which are almost round in shape, and sometimes I got very close to the elk. They became quite tame. I had no almanac, and lost all track of the days of the month, or of the week. All three of us pulled through the winter. I have never killed, at any time, more game or fish than was actually needed for food.

I was well known in Jackson Hole and the surrounding country, and was called "the Kid," "the Texas Kid," or occasionally, "the Montana Kid." Once I met a cowpuncher in Trinidad, Colorado, who was known as "the Texas Kid."

He was about my age. I do not remember his name. He told me his folks came up from Texas when he was quite young. He was nicknamed "the Texas Kid" at school and started cowpunching at an early age and the nickname stayed with him. He was a good-looking man and rated A-1 among cowpunchers. I was introduced to a "Montana Kid" in Los Angeles. He was a lightweight prize fighter. I think his name was Ogelsvie. Years later I met a character known as "Kid Tex" in Prince Rupert, British Columbia. His range was in the northwest, principally British Columbia. As a trapper and prospector he came to town about twice a year, there, during his sober moments, he was surrounded by a crowd of children whom he liked very much and bought candy, cold drinks, and ice cream. After starting ranching in Montana about 1895, I dropped the name of "Kid" as much as I could and was only known as such by a few old-time friends.

While mining in the vicinity of Dealth Valley about 1907, a union organizer came to my camp. A majority of my men did not want to join the union. I put the organizer out of camp on foot. The union must have traced me back to Montana, for shortly the news was passed around the camp that I was "the Texas Kid" or "the Montana Kid." I was not bothered any more by union organizers.

About this time in my career, while in the Hole, I found it necessary to wear at least one six-shooter where it could not be seen; for while it sometimes seemed to me to be a bit cowardly to do so, self-preservation is the first law of nature. I packed a sawed-off .45 in a light scabbard, inside my shirt in front at the belt-buckle location. The shirt was split down the front to give easy and quick access to the gun, and the scabbard was sewed to my underwear. It was quite common among gunmen and sheriffs at that time to carry one pistol upside down in a scabbard under the arm, with the gun hanging by the front sight. There was no draw-ing to it. You simply reached under your coat, flipped out your pistol, and fired from your stomach. It was all very quickly done. I seldom wore a coat; hence, the split shirt. There were no shirts on the market in those days open in front all the way down. The idea was my own.

When you have gained a reputation, whether you deserve it or not, guilty or not guilty, very often some rattle-brained fellow, especially when he is drinking, will get it into his head that he wants to kill you. At the least provocation he will start a quarrel, thinking, I presume, that the quarrel justifies his act. Now when you see that the fellow has nothing in his mind except to murder you and the psycho-logical moment has arrived, you beat him to the draw by a fraction. That is my only excuse for being here and able to tell you this tale. Anyway, by carrying one concealed gun I saved at least two men from being shot. By beating them to the draw, I was able to talk them out of the idea of shoot-ing me. A fraction of a second sometimes separates us from his life and eternity.

I liked the five-and-one-half-inch gun. It could be drawn quicker from the scabbard on the belt. Any gun of a smaller caliber than a .44 will not knock a man down when he is drinking or in anger. If you shoot a man with a small-caliber pistol he will keep on coming and probably shoot you.

My companions in the Hole at this time were Ed Hunter, Jack Shives, Joe Calhoun, John Cherry, Tom Tucker, Skeet-er, Cap Carson, Black Jack Foster, and others. They were a dependable bunch, and would stay "put." Nearly all of these boys took part in the so-called "Indian War" with me, and a few of them were with me when Owen Wister came in. I think I could name the boy who developed into "the Virginian." Most of these boys drifted into Alaska during the gold excitement, and I never heard of many of them again.

By this time almost all of the respectable bank robbers were trying to go straight. There were not many out-of-the-way places left. Settlements had claimed the West. However, the Curry-Cassidy gang was going strong, holding up trains and robbing banks in a very reckless manner. They had been given what you might term a "clear field." The others had scattered and gone.

One fall some of the boys living in the Hole saw that they had better get out for provisions before the trails all closed with snow too deep to travel through with horses. Five of them left the Hole with eight head of horses, with empty pack saddles on them. They went into Idaho, to a good-sized town on Snake River, at night, and broke into the general store. Two of the men remained in the street while the others loaded the eight horses with provisions. Only one citizen came along while the robbery was going on, and he was made to keep quiet until the party was gone.

There was a bag of peanuts lying on the floor, about the size of a small bed tick. They cut it open and on leaving filled their pockets with peanuts. The horses were not packed heavily, and a diamond hitch was thrown over each pack. On leaving, they hit a high lope and made nearly as good time as though they had no packs on their horses. A pack put on properly with a diamond hitch will stay there about as long as the horse's hide will stay on him.

About daylight they started up Trail Creek, which led into the mountains from Teton Basin. There was no turning-off place on the way into Jackson Hole over the top of the Teton Mountains, and there was no road at this time up Trail Creek.

When they started up the creek they began to eat peanuts

and drop the shells. It was learned later that the sheriff with a few deputies had followed them until they struck the peanut shells, then decided to go back. They seemed to interpret the shells as a trap which might lead them into a fight. Anyway, the posse knew that the destination of the robbers had to be Jackson Hole.

The sheriff and two deputies came back later across the southwest corner of the Yellowstone Park as far as the west side of Buffalo Fork, and camped. The bunch in the Hole knew when he came and I was asked to go up and hold a conversation with him by hollering across the river, which I did.

I asked the sheriff: "Are you the sheriff who is looking for the boys that got the peanuts?"

He shouted back that he was up the river camping and fishing a little. I then inquired what he was fishing for, saying that Buffalo Fork was running high.

"Yes," he replied, "but we thought . . . ." The rest was lost in the wind. I cut him off then, and told him we did not want to know what he thought but what the boys did want to know was whether he was coming or going. He said he was going. He left for Idaho the next morning.

Three of us made a trip into the Yellowstone National Park that winter on snowshoes, and pulled a sled. We went just for the fun of doing something, and halfway expected a little scrap out of the soldiers who were riding line there. We killed a bull buffalo near Fire Hole Basin; we brought his hide and head back to the Hole. We never saw any soldiers. That spring we let a fellow, who said his name was Lippincott and that he was a lawyer from Butte, Montana, take the head out to have it mounted. I never saw him or the head again.

One fall two boys came into the Hole with about sixty

57

head of stolen horses, mostly from Madison County, Montana. Their names were Spencer and Bernett; both of them were nearly dead from disease. Neither of them cared very much whether he lived or not. They had a hard time putting the horses through the winter. Toward spring it was necessary to beat trail across the flats to some ridges where the snow had blown off the grass in order to keep them from starving. The snow that winter was about five feet deep, packed solid. They camped at the head of Jackson Lake. During that spring word came up from the post office at Marysvale that the sheriff from Madison County, Montana, was there and was coming up for them. He added several settlers from the south end of the Hole to his posse. The boys could have easily gotten away but did not care to do so.

Spencer and Bernett were stopping that night in a cabin with myself and a friend. In the morning my friend went to the spring for water, which was about two hundred feet from the cabin, and was there held up by a squaw man, who was part of the sheriff's posse, which had surrounded the cabin. We both knew the squaw man; his name was John Carnes. My companion would not put his hands up for the squaw man, and proceeded to cuss him out. He then called for me to come out, which I did as I knew by that time that we were surrounded by the posse. We then went back a little way and sat down on a rock. Spencer and Bernett had two horses saddled and tied in a small log barn, and in a short time one of the boys from the cabin shot at a hat or something that was stuck up over a rock, and the ball opened. The posse almost riddled the cabin with bullets.

There was a man in the posse named Mose Giltner, who was standing behind the corner of the barn, at the far side of the round corral, peeping through the corral poles. One of the boys in the cabin must have seen him and shot. The bullet drove a splinter, about five inches long and bigger than a lead pencil, from one of the fir poles through the fellow's nose, and left it sticking out on both sides. He immediately gave a fair imitation of a Zulu war dance. I helped to extract the splinter when the fuss was over.

In a short time Spencer and Bernett seemed to have gotten tired of it in the cabin. One of them made a run for the barn and fell dead about halfway. The other one followed in a few seconds and was riddled with bullets and fell almost across the other one. I helped the sheriff gather what horses we could find, and he left that same day. He seemed to be in a hurry to leave. We buried Spencer and Bernett that evening.

One spring, when I returned from a bear hunt to my cabin on Crystal Creek, I noticed that the weeds and grass had been tramped down some, and my horse began to show signs of smelling something. I had just pulled a rifle from the scabbard which was under my leg when a big female mountain lion jumped up into a hole which had been cut for a window in the cabin. She sat in the window a few seconds before jumping out, and I realized by the way she was shed off on the stomach that she had little ones, and I did not shoot her. She ran away. I went inside and found two little ones, which did not have their eyes open yet. They were under my bunk so I let them alone, and went up the creek about a mile and camped. When I came back the next morning the kittens were gone. I presume that, catlike, she had carried them away.

The Crystal Creek cabin finally passed out of the Jackson Hole picture. About two thousand elk died of hunger in the snow on Crystal Creek one winter, and I had gotten about three or four hundred very superior elk teeth. They were kept in cans in the cabin. I had allowed a fellow whom I didn't know very well to make his home with me. Upon my return from a trip one day I found the cabin burned to the ground. I panned the ashes, about where the teeth ought to have been, but found no sign of them. I rode over three hundred miles to Livingston, Montana, on the trail of the thief, but learned that he had boarded a train a few hours before I got there. The teeth were gone; so was my cabin and so was the thief. He had just barely missed having a pleasant half-hour.

CHAPTER EIGHT

THE WILD BUNCH COMES A CALLING

THE HOLE IN THE WALL was far to the east of Jackson Hole and quite a difficult place to get into. It was necessary to go up a steep, rocky gorge and the last part of the way was between high, vertical, rock walls. Some of the trail was in a swift, roaring creek, which became Powder River. It was several miles in extent and from two to three miles across from the rimrocks to rimrocks. Quite a bunch of stock could be wintered there; a good portion of the territory grew a fine quality of bunch grass. A number of cattle rustlers lived in the vicinity.

The "Hole in the Wall gang" was what one might call the younger set. Generally they were much younger men and not so experienced in the holdup game as the Jackson Hole crowd, but they made more noise. I met several of these boys around the Curry ranch in the Little Rockies, Montana, before they had become known in the holdup racket. They worked off and on as cowpunchers, but were looked upon as cattle rustlers. Flat Nose George Curry, whose ranch was near the Big Horn Mountains in Wyoming, was a companion of theirs and his ranch was a hide-out for the gang.

I took a liking to one of these boys who went by the name of Maxwell, but he told me that his real name was Cassidy. He was called "Butch," was a quiet, unassuming fellow, and had a lot of "savvy." He came into the Hole about the middle of the nineties on what might be called a recruiting trip, that is, he was filling up the gaps in the ranks of the Hole in the Wall gang. A tall fellow called "Long Boy" came in with him.

Others of the gang that I knew were Ben Kilpatrick, a tall, splendid-looking fellow, Bill Carver, Comelio (Nancy) Hanks, Johnnie James, and Kid Curry. Flat Nose George Curry and Butch Cassidy were usually much in evidence when the gang was planning something.

Kid Curry (Harvey Logan) and some of the boys had murdered Pike Landusky in northern Montana, and later killed W. H. Winters, a cattleman from the same district who had been mixed up in the Landusky trouble. Two of Kid Curry's brothers had been killed prior to this time. The Jackson Hole crowd held themselves aloof from the noisy bunch on the east. When these men changed locations they also changed their names.

Shortly after the Hole in the Wall had become a real rendezvous, several of these men went to the eastward in the spring, and held up the Belle Fourche bank in Belle Fourche, South Dakota, securing about thirty thousand dollars. There was no one hurt, and it seemed an easy way to get money. In thirty or forty days they were all back in the Hole planning other holdups.

According to the newspapers and outside talk, these people were known as the "Kid Curry gang." That was not so. The Kid was young and had been in the vicinity but a very short time. There were several older men in the business who always took the leading part.

Black Jack Ketchum was quite a leader, and was well thought of by most of the men. Skeeter, Cassidy, Calhoun, Flat Nose, and others were listened to when they were "making medicine," and details were being gone over. Usually from three to six men took part in a holdup.

Kid Curry was not a favorite, and as he was constantly being hunted by the law, he had to keep moving. When planning something, several men always took part in the discussion. If any one of them seemed better qualified for the leadership of the particular job on hand, he was placed in charge. After all the plans had been made, I never knew one of them to disobey orders.

During the summer that the Belle Fourche bank was robbed, a Union Pacific train was held up at Wilcox, Wyoming, and another, at Tipton, Wyoming; and a bank at Winnemucca, Nevada, was robbed and about twenty-five thousand dollars taken. Soon after that a bank at Montpelier, Idaho, was relieved of nearly thirty-five thousand dollars, and several other robberies were charged to the gang. Their last real job however, was the holdup of a Great Northern train, near Wagner, Montana, when they got about ninety thousand dollars.

The Hole in the Wall gang made us a visit one spring. They were a loud-talking bunch and told us of a humorous incident of a recent holdup. We had quite a laugh over it. They had held up a train somewhere in Nevada and were going through the passengers in the day coach. The man doing the collecting was passing through the day coach with a small gripsack, which he held open. There was a man on guard in each end of the coach. About the center of the car was a woman who would not keep still and was giving a little trouble. When the collector got to her she spit in his face.

He poked her a little with the barrel of his six gun and she immediately collapsed, and went into a faint. You can never tell what a woman will do.

I never cared much for any of that crowd. I am speaking now about the boys from the Hole in the Wall. They were a good deal on the roughneck order, and some of them were killers. The difference between a killer and the commonly called gunman was that the killer would take advantage of one in a gun fight, such as shooting a man in the back; a gunman aimed to give a fellow a fair break. If you didn't want to fight you didn't have to, but if you started to draw and were killed it was considered a fair fight. In the case of the killer, it always looked to me as though one called two. The more men he put away the more there were looking for him. He never lived to be very old.

For about fourteen years I never took my guns off, night or day, so to speak. When I laid off my guns, the feeling, I presume, was similar to that of women when they quit wearing corsets. I felt a goneness.

CHAPTER NINE

"THE SHERIFFS WERE DODGING ME"

THE RUSTLER'S WAR BROKE OUT fresh again in Johnson County, Wyoming, after the fight at the Champion ranch. Several of us in Jackson Hole went down and hooked up with the cow interests for a while but did not like it much and started back toward the Hole country, feeling rather sore. A couple of our friends had been shot. We blamed the sheep interests for the loss of our friends, and we did considerable damage to the bands of sheep we met on our way back.

There had been trouble in Johnson County for many years. Our only interest was to even up the score for the shooting of our friends. I have heard it said that our crowd were paid killers financed by the cattle interests. I don't think that was true. I never knew a man who received any such pay. I was acquainted with Tom Horn, but did not agree with the people who hung him in Cheyenne.

As we approached one band of sheep near the head of Green River, the herder became frightened and stampeded, going as hard and as fast as he could run for the thick willows which grew next to the river. We gave chase and roped him just as he was going into the brush. We took him to his camp where we ate up most of his grub, then put his sheep into Green River, and set him afoot. Our interests, if we had any, were with cattle. There was never much sympathy shown for sheepmen or sheepherders.

Rendezvous or hide-outs were seldom used by outlaws unless they had homesteads there. An outlaw's safety lay in traveling around. He spent a good deal of his time working in mining or cow camps and in small towns loafing, gambling, and drinking hooch or tending bar. Cattle rustlers usually hung around some small ranch where the owner was not so particular whose calf he put his brand on. There was a vast social barrier between a high-class bank robber and the ordinary cattle rustler and holdup man.

The Roundup Association made such a close inspection of brands and marks that it was almost impossible to ship stolen beef. However, there were always some stolen cattle sold to local butchers or to railroad construction camps. Most of a rustler's activities were on unbranded calves, or getting rations from an Indian agency and selling them. That class of thieves never had much money. I think that must have caused the social barrier.

I have known men who were classed as outlaws, whom I had more respect for than for some Indian agents and their assistants. I mean those agents who would sell the Indian's rations to ranchers, cowpunchers, and prospectors. This would cut the Indians short on grub. I have known Indian Department cattle to be butchered and sold to railroad construction camps and the meat replaced for the Indians with big-jaw cattle. Big jaws are diseased cattle that could not be shipped or sold to white folks.

The so-called leader of a band of outlaws was not necessarily a rough, domineering person. In order to hold the respect of this class of man the first and most important

66

things were honesty, square dealing with all the men, plenty of common sense, and also a good nerve and ability to make good whenever necessary. No tricking, double-crossing, or shortchanging was permitted by him. A man who was crooked with his companions did not live to be old.

There had been a bank robbed in northern Wyoming, and about twenty thousand dollars had been secured by the bandits. Most of the money was for the crop of wool that was being sold. The outlaws rode westward all the afternoon and until after midnight, and it looked as though they were not being followed. They had gone to a cabin where one man lived alone. The cabin was about thirty feet long, and the west end had no floor, making a good place to stand horses. The cabin stood on a bench about one hundred yards back from the bluff of a big creek. The bluff was about one hundred feet high and shaped like a horseshoe. The cabin faced the bluff to the south while behind it, about fifty yards away, there was a little bluff, about twenty or thirty feet high, going onto flat benchlands. About one hundred feet to the east there was a bunch of bushes and a spring.

All the horses were taken into the cabin, fed hay and oats, and all hands went to sleep. There was a door in the front and one at the back of the cabin. When the owner of the place went to the spring in the morning just before sunrise, he was held up by two of the posse which had the cabin surrounded. In a short time they opened fire, but their shooting at the outlaws did not do a great deal of damage.

The outlaws would expose themselves at the back of the cabin, trying to draw fire from the low benchlands on the north. Soon they knew they were guarded only on two sides and from the little branch running from the spring and behind the creek bank to the south. The posse must have reached there about daybreak, and did not know the lay of the land, or they would have posted guards on all sides of the cabin. Possibly none of them cared to be exposed on the open benchlands to the north; there was no bank there to get behind.

After exchange of a good many shots one of the outlaws on his horse made a run from the cabin for the benchlands. The attention of the posse was attracted by the ones in the cabin, who made it so interesting for the posse that there were only one or two shots fired at him. He told me later that he shot at the man at the spring and saw where the bullet had hit the ground in front of his face. The man didn't return the fire.

It is odd how you will notice some of the little details during a time like that. One of the bandits told me that he noticed two of the guns fired by the posse would penetrate the logs—some of the bullets falling to the floor and others sticking in the opposite wall. The cabin was built of dry fir logs, about ten by twelve inches through, very hard wood. One bullet went through the top of a coffee-pot which was on the stove; another struck a picture on the wall. Five horses were standing in the west end and none were hit.

By making a little circular ride on the bench, the man who left the cabin swung around and came back up on the west side of the horseshoe curve. Leaving his horse out of the sight of the posse, he crawled up to the edge of the high cut bank, draging a .30–30 rifle with him. He could see the men lying on their stomachs against the cut bank; they had not seen him. He opened fire among them as fast as he could shoot, not wanting to hit anyone. They ran, rolled, tumbled, and did everything they could to get out of there. The men in the side branch did the same, and joined their companions. The men from the cabin ran to the edge of the bluff but, by this time, there was no one left to shoot at. I do not think there was anyone hit by a bullet in the whole affair.

The posse had left their horses around the bend, down the creek, out of sight; otherwise they probably would have been set afoot. The boys now came back to the cabin, while the owner of the cabin stayed on the bluff, acting as a lookout. They cooked and ate their breakfast and rode away on a walk.

The bandits soon split up, part of them going north to Montana, and the rest into Jackson Hole. They had very little fear of further pursuit. I was asked the question once, if that was the time I was dodging sheriffs. I replied; "No, that was the time sheriffs were dodging me."

I was riding alone one morning in a northerly direction. I had just heard that a bank had been robbed at Montpelier, Idaho, the day before. About that time I discovered that I was being followed by a small posse of about four men. I eased along for a little while when I realized that it had developed into a chase. I did not want to be questioned by these men, and I did not want to do any shooting. By their actions I understood that they wanted to catch up with me. Anyhow, when I heard a bullet go by, instead of stopping, I went into a real run. I was not long in losing them for I had the fastest horse; besides, I was very light riding and could make a horse last for a long distance. After I was sure that they were lost I turned at right angles, going nearly due west into the mountains and toward the Union Pacific Railroad. Just before sundown I fetched up on a mountain side, in a patch of timber, about two miles from a small town on the railroad. I unsaddled my horse and cached my saddle, together with my hat, boots, spurs, and guns, except one .45 which I wore high under my left arm in a scabbard.

I wore a small felt hat, a very common coat, and low-heeled shoes. My cordouroy pants still showed the crease where they had been worn inside of my high-heeled boots, but they would soon straighten out.

I led my horse down to a small creek and washed all the saddle marks and dust off him and turned him loose. By morning when his hair was dry, you could not tell that he had been ridden. Then I walked to the railroad. It was now about one hour after dark. The first train that pulled in was a freight which stopped for water. I walked alongside of the train until I came to a boxcar with one door open, which already had some hobos in it, and I climbed in. Two of the boys were of the thug type, and appeared to be pretty rough. The others were ranch hands just going somewhere.

After the train pulled out one of the boys said to me: "We paid the brakeman one dollar apiece to ride in here, and it's now your turn to pay us." After a light argument I gave them one dollar, but in doing so they heard some more silver rattle in my pockets. Their actions from that time on told me that they intended to rob me before I got away. I sat on the opposite side of the car from the open door on the floor, with my back against the other door. After several hours' time we pulled into the railroad yards at Pocatello, Idaho. There was an electric light near by which made it quite light. Just before the train stopped one boy lightly slapped his hand against my pants pocket and satisfied himself that there was more silver there. I had considerable money on my person which I didn't want to part with.

As the train made its last bump, one of them jumped out; the other sat in the door with his legs hanging out. I also sat down in the door. As I jumped I pulled my .45. As I hit the ground I jabbed the fellow who was already out as hard as I could in the stomach with the barrel of the gun and

70

jumped back away from him. Just as the other one hit the ground I had them both covered and told them if they started anything I would kill them and that I was going uptown and did not want them to follow me. One of the fellows said: "Tell me where you got that gat." I told him I was a magician, and got it out of the air. I then went up through the railroad yards into town to a rooming house and went to bed. By the second or third day I was there, I had bought a suit of clothes and a railroad ticket to the Pacific Coast.

In about sixty days time I was back in the town near where I had turned my horse loose. I hired a saddle horse and rode out to a ranch which was about five miles' distance from my cache. At the ranch were three grown boys who knew the near-by range well. I described my horse marks and brands, and asked them if they had seen him. They said they had and knew where he was running with a small band of horses. I told them he was my horse, and I would give them ten dollars to bring him in. I remained at the ranch, and in about two hours' time my horse was in the corral. I gave one of the boys a dollar for a grass rope, built a hackmore on the horse, and led him away. My cache was just as I left it. After putting my rig on my horse, I led him to the edge of town and tied him there until I returned the hired horse; then I walked back to my own horse and rode away, still wearing my store clothes.

CHAPTER TEN

THE STORY OF A BANK ROBBERY

I HAVE NEVER SEEN a robber's own description of a bank robbery in print, so I will try to tell this one just as he told it to me. In case any one of the trio ("John," "Jack," and "Joe," we will call them) should ever be serving time, I will try to have the story published by some magazine so it may bring him in a little tobacco money. You can take it for what it is worth. The last time I heard from Joe he sent me Shakespeare's complete works, leather bound, from England.

The three boys were very much attached to each other and were honorable, in their way, and I know, would have stayed together in any kind of mix-up. They were the kind of men that were not afraid of the devil, and there were no better or quicker shots in the entire country. None of them ever had any desire to kill anyone and were very reluctant to shoot a man under any provocation.

They had the respect of everyone that knew them. None of them were large men; Jack was the tallest, about five feet, nine inches, with straight brown hair and rather rosy complexion when not badly tanned. Joe was very slim and about five feet, seven, with dark complexion, very dark hair and eyes. He was quite well educated and very fond of poetry. He had traveled abroad. John was the shortest of the three, about five feet, six inches tall, weighing about 140 pounds, of rather light complexion. If John had any personal characteristic, it was in singing songs. You just could not keep him from singing.

They were not the roughneck type and all were very moderate drinkers. All were good riders and very fond of horses. They looked upon bank-robbing as a pastime that put pep into life. It was not considered very bad to rob a bank in the West during that time. There was always a fascination in the long quiet night rides. I never knew of a bank's closing its doors on account of being robbed, and I never could make out who lost the money that was stolen. The depositors kept on drawing checks as though nothing had happened.

It was the year of 1893 or '94. Quite a spectacular bank robbery was pulled off in a small town about fifty miles south of Salt Lake City, just at the noon hour, without a shot's being fired. The bank was on a corner, and down the side street from the corner and just behind the bank building was a saloon with a hitching rail for horses in front. Between the bank building and the saloon was an alley. The bandits rode into town one at a time from different directions. They had the appearance of cowboys or ranchers, with silk scarfs around their necks. The first man to arrive rode up to the hitching rail, dropped his reins over the top of the post at the end of the rack, and sat down on the steps in front of the saloon.

In about two minutes the second man arrived and dropped the reins of his horse's bridle over the same post, and started to work with one of the stirrup leathers on his saddle. He

73

didn't speak to, or notice, the other man. When the third man came in sight about a block away, the second man walked down the alley behind the bank and came around the block, which put him in front of the bank coming from the opposite direction. On the arrival of the third man, the first man got up and slowly sauntered along the side of the bank building, the third man following a short distance behind.

There were very few people on the street, and no one suspicioned anything. The three men met in front of the bank and pulled their neck scarfs up over their noses. One quickly stepped up to the cashier's window, another took possession of two citizens who were at the counter. The first words were: "Hands up. Don't make any noise or you will be shot."

One of the bandits, who had stepped up on a chair inside the door, kept up a continuous conversation along the lines of: "Keep still. No false moves and no one will be hurt. We mean to rob this bank but don't want to shoot anyone."

There were only three employees in the bank. One citizen came in while the holdup was going on. He was lined up with the others. They were all put behind the counter against the wall and made to sit down. One of the bandits with a seamless sack gathered up all the money he could find; the safe was standing open. He later told me he got over twelve thousand dollars. The man who gathered up the coin was the last to leave the bank. The sack was passed to one of the others who left at once for his horse. The last one remained in the bank for several seconds and slowly backed out. Before the alarm was given the trio was out of sight and, as far as they knew, there was never any pursuit from town; not a shot was fired.

That afternoon, they were coming up along the west side

of a valley about a mile wide, riding northeast next to the foothills, about thirty-five miles south of Salt Lake City. It was nearly sundown. It had begun to look to them like a clean getaway. They were just passing the mouth of a gulch, which came in from the west, with a road coming down it, when they saw a cloud of dust up the gulch and some horsemen riding in their direction.

The country was full of cattlemen doing roundup work. The bandits could not tell whether it was a posse on their trail, trying to head them off, or whether it was cattlemen. They spurred up to a fast run, but were not long in doubt. The posse came out of the gulch on a dead run and opened fire at about a quarter of a mile's distance. One of the bandits was carrying a forty-five caliber, center-fire, Winchester takedown rifle, the only rifle in the party. It had just appeared on the market about a year before. A takedown gun could be carried behind the cantle of a saddle, rolled up with a few other necessary things in a slicker, and not be seen while riding through the country.

The way the posse crowded them they evidently thought there were only six-shooters to compete with. The outlaws' horses were not fresh as they had been ridden fairly hard. The outlaw with the rifle was riding a thoroughbred, which was still in fine shape, so he fell behind, as sort of a rear guard.

The posse came up to within about three hundred yards of the trio, riding two abreast and very close together. Their bullets were going by pretty lively. The man with the rifle turned around and opened fire, knocking down two of their horses in a few seconds' time. The posse immediately scattered: some started up the hillside, some went into the dry creek bed that ran along on the right, where they got off of their horses and hid behind the bank which was about two

75

feet high. When John, the bandit with the rifle, saw what they were doing he turned to join his companions.

About seventy-five or one hundred yards ahead of him he saw Joe on the ground trying to get up. His horse was loose going across the flat in a run, and quartering broadside to the posse. It was useless to try to catch the horse. By the time he got to Joe, he was standing on his feet, but was badly hurt. The bullet had struck him just under the right shoulder blade and had come out just above the right breast, tearing a big hole. John had succeeded in getting him on his horse when Jack came riding back. He handed Jack his rifle and a handful of cartridges, and climbed on his horse behind Joe. During this time the bullets were hitting the ground around them, and going over and by them aplenty, but no one was hurt. Jack fired a few shots which seemed to have a quieting effect.

The bandits then ran across the flats in a northeast direction to a gulch which had a trail going up it, and where they were not in much danger of being headed off by another posse. They had been over that route before. The posse didn't crowd the bandits on this flat but shot at them at long range all the way across, without doing any damage. Jack did not waste much ammunition on them.

About a half a mile up from the mouth of the gulch was a ledge of rocks which came down to the bottom of it. Below the ledge was about a quarter of a mile of straight, flat ground, while above this point to the top of the range the trail was quite crooked. It was sundown now. John had given Jack more cartridges for his rifle, and when they got to the ledge Jack got off his horse and cached himself and his horse behind the rocks. The posse came within sight in three or four minutes—two of them about one hundred yards in advance of the rest. Jack said he let the first two come up within less than one hundred yards of him, then killed both horses. One horse fell on the rider's leg and held him, laying with his back toward Jack. He could hear him crying for mercy. The other fellow took straight back down the gulch as fast as he could run. With every shot over his head fired at the balance of the posse, the fellow would leap into the air and yell. Jack joined the other two boys a little later near the top of the range. He never knew what damage he had done to the posse, and never saw any more of them.

By nine or ten o'clock that night John's horse began to show signs of strain of the carrying double, although they were both small men. Joe was quite weak by this time. The bandits pulled off to one side of the road and stopped for about half an hour, and ate some dried elk meat. There was less than a pint of whiskey with the outfit, and this was kept for Joe.

It was during this stop that they decided to take Joe back to Salt Lake City, as they didn't believe he could get well without the service of a good doctor and good care. There was nothing of that kind in the direction they were going. They separated here, Jack going northeast, Joe and John going west. It looked like the "Devil take care of his own."

They had something like twenty-five miles to ride and were all night making the trip. They came into the main street of the city when it just began to show daylight in the east. John had gotten off the horse and Joe was just able to sit on him. They heard a wagon coming and John stepped into the street and stopped it. It was a Chinaman with a load of vegetables. John explained his trouble and they put Joe on the wagon seat, while John got on his horse and lead the way to a livery stable which he knew about. The big doors were open and the wagon was driven into the barn. They unloaded the wounded man and handed the Chink

77

ten dollars. He backed out of the barn and was soon out of sight down the street.

They removed as much clothing from Joe as could be spared, together with his belt, six-shooter, spurs, money, and hat. The stableman and John then put him into a hack and took him to a first-class hospital. John didn't go into the hospital as his clothing was very bloody, but he gave the stableman five hundred dollars to leave at the hospital as a guarantee or part payment, as the case might be. He told the stableman to say that they did not want any unnecessary publicity, but what they did want was good medical care.

John got out of the hack in front of a clothing store, that was just opening up at sunrise, and about half an hour later he came out of there with a complete change of hand-me-down clothing from his shoes to his hat. All of his old clothes were carried in a bundle.

There is no better disguise than a suit of hand-me-down clothes. John then returned to the stable where he made arrangements for washing his horse, saddle, and clothing, then went to a rooming house and went to bed. He paid liberally for his clothes and at the stable, having found out that liberal use of money is a good way to keep most people from asking questions.

About eleven o'clock that morning, the stableman came to his room and told him his partner was doing fine. He continued sleeping all day and night.

The next day he made his first visit to the hospital and spent a few hours listening to street talk and reading newspapers. The first paper he saw stated that the posse had had a running fight and that one of the outlaw's arms was broken. It said that the robbers were closely pursued, and that the place had been found where the wounds had been dressed and where the bandits had secured a change of horses. This was mostly due to the propaganda which Jack had left along the way. John made up his mind that everything was all right, and decided to remain in the city.

He went to a tailor shop and ordered two up-to-date suits of clothes. In a week's time he was rigged out from hat to shoes, moved to a good hotel and spent a pleasant five weeks in the city. He got well acquainted with some of the nurses in the hospital and occasionally took one or two of them to the show, or sometimes horseback riding in the evenings. Jack came in about three weeks later and spent a few days there. Joe's recovery was rapid, and in five weeks' time he and John rode out of Salt Lake City.

CHAPTER ELEVEN

THE JACKSON HOLE INDIAN WAR

IN THE SUMMER OF 1895, I got mixed up in the Jackson Hole Indian war. Some of the Mormon boys from the lower end of the Hole came up where several of us were camped and informed us that there was a massacre planned by the Indians from the eastward. There had been considerable friction for some time between the settlers of the Hole and the Indians over the killing of elk and antelope in the Hole by the Indians.

The information came from a cowboy named Jim Lanagan, who lived on the Gros Ventre River with a squaw man named Carnes. The Shoshonis, Arapahoes, Bannocks, and a few visiting Indians were in the country and wanted to fight. They had been listening to the old bucks telling them about the good old days when white men's scalps hung from their belts. Young bucks are easily excited by that kind of talk. The settlers asked us if we would help them, which we consented to do.

There were about ten of us, and I was asked to take a part as leader of the bunch. I at once sent out some small scouting parties. On their return, two or three days later, they reported plenty of Indians in the hills (especially on the headwaters of the Green River, Grays River, and the Gros Ventre). They said that the Indians were sullen and didn't want any white men around, and that a prospector had been killed.

We called a sort of mass meeting and organized. I was elected captain. The women, children, and a few old men were moved into Bishop Wilson's house, which was something on the order of a stockade, in the lower end of the Hole. Bishop Wilson was a Mormon. Our force at various times mustered forty to sixty men. We were indeed a rough-looking set. Several of us wore buckskin shirts and almost all carried, besides rifles, one or two six-shooters.

We used very few pack horses, traveled light, and were successful in surprising most of the Indians.

To a man who does not know Indians this surrounding and surprising them may sound simple, but to a man who knows, it's different. Each Indian camp has a lookout at some advantageous place where he can see everything from a coyote to a horse as soon as it appears on the horizon. The lookout is wrapped in a blanket up to his eyes and you cannot see him. He has various ways of signaling to the camp. In sunshiny weather it is usually with a looking glass: in cloudy weather, a blanket or smoke. Lookouts are usually small boys.

My knowledge of Indians was a great help. With a good pair of field glasses I kept well ahead of our outfit and made close inspections from all ridges and high places. After the Indians were located we stayed several miles away until after dark, then moved up closer. We always first found their horse herd, and generally had them surrounded at daybreak. An Indian on foot is not hard to handle, and we brought them in without a fight. We would round up a bunch, bring them into the Hole, and camp them among some big cottonwood trees at the Rhodes cabin. Rhodes was a justice of the peace. He was a tubercular, and had come there for his health. We put the Indians under arrest, put a herder with their horses, and a guard with the prisoners. We fed and took good care of them.

After the second or third trip we were getting short of ammunition, so we sent a Norwegian out with a list of the various calibers of cartridges that we needed. They were from .30–30 Winchester to .45–75 bottleneck, besides the six-shooter shells. I don't know what he told on the outside, but from that time on, what the newspapers in the East printed was aplenty. For example, I later got hold of a New York paper with a full-page picture, showing a cabin among some very tall pine trees with Indians tied to the trees and cowpunchers scalping them. In big type it read: "CRAWFORD'S CABIN" and "ONLY HOUSE IN JACKSON'S HOLE."

There were very few casualties during the trouble. One white man was wounded and several horses were killed. In about a month's time we had the Indians' plans pretty well broken up. Our last trip we came back without any Indians. It happened something like this: Indians were getting hard to find and were pretty well scattered through the hills. We would first locate the Indians with a small scouting party before taking our main body of men into the mountains. On this last scouting trip, I was accompanied by a sheriff and two men.

We were riding a trail on the mountain side. About one hundred feet above us and to the left was a small flat benchland which we could not see. There was a fusilade of shots on this bench. I counted forty shots. The mountain side was too steep to get a horse up so I left my horse and scrambled up on hands and knees. I was met at the rim of the bench by an Indian who covered me with his rifle but didn't shoot. From where I stood I could see eight or ten Indians on the ground beginning to cut up the elk they had just killed.

I knew then that they were a war party or they would have sent the squaws for the meat. The Indian said to me: "How many of you."

I said forty or fifty.

"You heap lie. Why not forty? Why not fifty? You heap lie. Where you from?"

I replied: "Jackson Hole."

"Jackson Hole heap no good. You go, no come back."

The Indian could not see down into the canyon from where I came from, and he was afraid to take a chance and go down there. None of the other men were with me. They were taking care of the sheriff who, strange as it may seem, had completely collapsed while the shooting was going on. We had all got off our horses. The sheriff came to me, put his hands on me, and begged me to take him back to Jackson Hole.

I cussed the fellow and kicked him trying to bring him back to his senses but it was no use. He was what you call frightened stiff. This happened about noon. We rode until the next morning at sunrise getting back to the Hole, and in about two hours' time were on our way with over fifty men to overtake the Indians. The next day we found where the hunting party had joined their main camp, and the next morning we had them surrounded before daylight, and cut off from their horses.

We took them without a fight, although we had to make considerable "medicine." They were very sullen and wanted to fight. There were two squaws with them. One of the Arapahoes told me he was a relative of Chief Little Raven

83

Head, who took part in the peace council at Medicine Creek, Kansas, in 1867, between the Plains Indians and the government. I was very favorably impressed with Little Raven Head and sent him to Fort Washakie with a letter to the Indian agent.

Amongst their paraphernalia they had a lot of elk meat already cut from the bones which we wanted to take with us for food. The meat made two very heavy packs. We packed up in a big hurry and started, for we knew there were some big war parties in the neighborhood. We crowded the Indians pretty fast but all morning the two squaws, who were looking after the pack horses, had trouble with the meat packs.

We finally stopped to repack. I was nearly dead for lack of sleep and left some of the boys in charge. I lay down and in a minute was sound asleep. In about thirty minutes I was awakened and saw a bunch of Indians with their heads together, "making medicine." Most of the white men were asleep. The Indians were talking with their hands and making no noise. Now when an Indian talks that way it's "bad medicine."

I scattered the Indians, waked the white men, and we soon got underway in this kind of formation: white man, Indian, white man, Indian. There was a white man between every two Indians and some times two of my men between the bucks, with a couple of whites behind the squaws with the packs.

Just before sundown we were on a narrow trail on the mountainside along Horse Creek, hurrying to get over the divide before dark. I didn't think it safe to remain overnight on the east side of the divide. All at once a terrific yell arose from the Indians and at least three pistol shots were fired. In packing up that morning we had searched the camp very carefully and thought we had all the firearms but had over-looked some pistols. The Indians dove into the timber on the upper side of the trail and scattered like that many quail. I was riding one of the Indians' horses, which was only half broken. We went off the trail on the low side and he tried to stampede down the mountain. When I got him headed in the right direction, a precious half-minute had been lost and there was not an Indian in sight. My horse was scarred along the side of his neck by a bullet from the Indian who rode behind me. The wound was bleeding quite freely. Most of the other boys were scattered through the timber, trying to see something to shoot at. A few shots were being fired.

The mountains opened up in a short distance to small open parks with no timber though a lot of tall grass. I spurred my horse until he could hardly jump, then went on foot. When near the upper end of a park I saw four legs of a horse standing in the edge of the small, thick timber. I was in about the center of one of the open parks. I must have made some little move that told the Indian I had seen him, and in a few seconds I saw a puff of white smoke and heard the bullet go by me. I shot at him just as he threw his left leg over the rump of his horse. He was getting on from the off-side. I saw that he was hit or wounded, and I quickly made into the timber but didn't shoot again. I walked slowly up to where he had been but he was gone. I tracked his horse a short distance and found a red and white blanket with considerable blood on it, which he had lost.

I started back, taking the blanket with me. All the shooting had stopped and I could not see a white man or Indian anywhere. I had reached the upper end of the park where I left my horse, when all at once I saw the black head of an Indian just at the top of the tall grass. I drew a bead on him and held it there a few seconds without shooting, thinking something must be wrong. Then I saw a small hand go up to the face.

One of the squaws had a small boy with her; he was about two or three years old. He was lost in the getaway and was standing there crying. I picked him up and started toward my horse, but the child pointed to the side of the park and wanted to go that way. I went a short distance with him and found an Indian lying there, badly wounded. He made me the sign for water. I put the boy down with him and brought water in my hat. I wanted to take him with me, but he told me by sign to let him stay there as the Indians knew where he was and would come back for him.

The Indian wore a medicine bag around his neck made from the skin of a magpie. I hope it carried him to the Happy Hunting Ground. He wore white man's pants with the seat cut out and had a hat with the crown cut out. His hat was off. He asked me to take off his pants as it was not good medicine for an Indian to die in white man's clothes. I removed his pants. His name was Like-a-Man.

I made him as comfortable as I could and covered him with the blanket but took the child with me. When I got down to the trail it was just dark and our crowd had all the Indian pack horses rounded up. We hurriedly unpacked them by cutting the latigo strings and turned them loose. No white man can untie Indian knots in the dark. We went over the divide and into camp for the night. My idea of turning the Indian horses loose was that if they came back for Like-a-Man, they would find some horses to get out on. We put all of their equipment in a pile and covered it with what canvas they had.

I do not think the Indian child waked up once during the night. He was all smiles in the morning and didn't ask for his mother, or say anything about the other Indians. He waded out into the nearly ice-cold creek and bathed himself all over, then came back to me and I wrapped him in a blanket. When we were packed up and ready to go, I stood him up in a rawhide pack bag, gave him a quirt, so he could whip his horse, and turned him loose with the pack horses.

We had, if I remember right, seventeen guns, several six-shooters and considerable ammunition which we had taken from the Indians. This we cached in the crevice of some near-by rocks. I never knew what became of any of it.

About noon the next day we were met by one of our horse wranglers from the camp in the Hole who informed us that an army officer, with several soldiers and an Indian agent, were at the Rhodes cabin and expected to put us under arrest. They had come on ahead of the company which were coming over the Teton Pass.

Now our idea of a court-martial trial was to be shot at sunrise, and we didn't particularly like the idea. We left our pack horses with one man where the Gros Ventre River comes out of the canyon into the Hole, and all rode in. In front of the Rhodes cabin we stopped in a half-circle. There were fifty-seven men in our party. The army officer in charge was Brigadier General Coppinger, U.S.A.

He stood in front of the cabin with several of his men. My position was about the center of the half-circle. The General stepped out toward me and asked for the captain. I don't know where he had learned my rank, but I replied: "I am him." I think the reason I was called "captain" was because it was easy to say.

He turned to a couple of his aides and told them to put me under arrest. In less time than it takes to tell, there were fifty-six guns thrown down on his small party. I motioned to the two men to back away from in front of my horse, which they did. I didn't pull a gun or offer any resistance.

87

However, I suggested to the General that we talk the matter over a little as the boys didn't seem to take to the idea of my being arrested.

The General's lips were trembling perceptibly, and I noticed that some of his men were white around the gills. The matter of my being put under arrest seemed to have been forgotten as there was no more said about it.

We "made medicine" around there for probably half an hour, and I don't remember that we reached any understanding about anything. We offered some of the Mormon boys to go with them, and give them all the information possible, and told the officers that we were men who would not be arrested at that particular time. Not, at least, while we were alive. However, we did agree to turn the rest of the Indian fighting over to the War Department as it was out of our line anyway. We had undoubtedly prevented a massacre of the settlers in the Hole. But it was hard to make the War Department see it that way. We were all in bad with them, and it was time to scatter.

The General's company was then bringing their paraphernalia over the Teton Mountains, coming into the Hole. There was quite a little talk among our boys about going over and ambushing the soldiers in the canyon; our boys were rearing for a fight. However, a few of us talked the matter down, and we rode back that evening to our packs, each man sorting out his little belongings, and there we separated. We decided that our part of the war was over and we didn't want to be around while the soldiers were there.

The next night, just before dark, I left Antelope Springs with one man and one pack horse for Montana by southwest Yellowstone Park, Henry's Lake, and Madison River trail. Dick Rock and Vic Smith were then living at Henry's

Lake, Idaho. They had a cow moose broken to drive. Vic Smith was rated as about the best two-gun man in those parts.

There was a family by the name of Dwellies living near there. The boys were hunters, and sometimes acted as guides for hunting parties. Two companions and myself stopped there one day when they had some eastern people with them. After leaving I spoke of the place as the Dude Ranch. I believe that was the coining of the name "dude ranch."

Speaking of pop shots that kill the devil: That night while riding through a sagebrush flat I heard an antelope, jumping stiff-legged, and thought he stopped. My horse stopped; it was real dark and I could see nothing. I shot with a six-shooter at where I thought he ought to be. Riding up I found him lying there, kicking, with his back broken.

The soldiers came on into the Hole and some of the Mormon boys acted as guides, taking them over our entire battlefield. They found the Indian, Like-a-Man, whom I had left on the mountain side, dead. The Indians never came back for him as he told me they would.

At a ford across a big creek, a few miles from there, they found the Indian I had shot while getting on his horse. He was shot through the hip and one arm was broken. He said he soon lost his horse after being hit and crawled about three miles to this ford, and was picked up there by the soldiers. He afterward recovered. His name was Ben Sinowine. It developed that he was the same Indian who rode behind me and wounded my horse in the neck. The little boy we left with the Indians in the Hole was afterward restored to his mother. I received all this information by mail while I was in Montana sometime later.

I was told some years later by an army officer who was with General Coppinger in the Hole that we were the toughest-looking bunch of men he had ever seen, and he complimented me on the discipline of the men, saying that I had them under wounderful control. This was General Switzer, and I met him at St. Andrews Bay, Florida.

I learned later that there had been a trial or an investigation of some kind at Cheyenne about the Indian trouble in the Hole. Ben Sinowine was there as a witness. I was told that he packed a six-shooter under his blanket all the time, looking for the man they called "Buckskin." That was me.

I still have two of the buckskin shirts trimmed with bear teeth and beaver, hanging in my cabin, which I wore over forty years ago in the Indian war. Luckily I was not there in Cheyenne at the investigation, as Ben lost the opportunity of making a target of himself.

When asked about the particular time when the Indians made the break on Horse Creek, Ben showed them the formation in which we rode by placing some pebbles in a row, and alternating them saying: "White man, Indian; white man, Indian." When asked if any horses were shot, he said, "No, white man no shoot horses, white man shoot Indians." As the Indians clung to their horses about as tight as horsehair and no horses were hit, it speaks well for our marksmanship.

CHAPTER TWELVE

OWEN WISTER VISITS THE HOLE

THINKING IT BEST to stay out of the States for a while, I fell in, one fall, with a small band of Cree Indians on Bow River, Canada, and decided to winter with them. These Indians, when talking to white folks, spoke a language called "Chinook." It was a language gotten up, I understand, by Hudson's Bay trappers. It didn't have many words in it, but they were very impressive. All of the northeast tribes spoke some of it.

The Cree Indians had taken part in Riel's Rebellion some years before, and were not given any rations by the Canadian government. It was hard scratching for them to get enough to eat. I had seven head of saddle horses. I went out to the settlement and brought in all the grub I could pack, together with some traps and strychnine. It was an unusually hard winter—lots of snow, cold, and several hard blizzards, without a single chinook. The cattle were all weak and began to die the latter part of February.

We had no horses strong enough to ride by this time, but I had pushed them down in some breaks along the river, where there was a little picking to be had, and it looked as though they would pull through. In the early winter, I had cached a part of my grub, but by this time the Indians had found it. There was nothing to do but help them eat it. By the first of March all of the store of grub was gone, my horses were too weak to ride, there was about a foot of crusted snow, and nearly all the time we had bad weather.

I had trapped all winter and had considerable fur— beaver, a few otters, some martens and ermine. In the early part of the winter I had gone as far north as the Red Deer River. I was now eating the same kind of food as the Indians were. The wolves were very fat, and the cattle very thin and also getting scarce and hard to find. We would take the fat from the poisoned wolves and cook the lean, tough beef with it. I traveled on homemade snow shoes. If you have never tried them you will not understand.

About April 1, I left there by myself, pulling a toboggan with my furs and all the belongings that I had left on it— namely, saddle, bridle, chaps and spurs, and my guns. The snow usually held me up until about the middle of the morning. After that it would be breaking through the rest of the day.

The grub was sometimes nothing. The last end of the trip it was jackrabbits. My snowshoes were worn out. My clothes were the kind made by a squaw, a mixture of cloth and buckskin. My shoes were a large pair of moccasins, pulled over what was left of a pair of cowpuncher's boots. If there is anything that will hold dirt and grease and smoke better than buckskin, I have not met it. My hair had not been cut during the winter. I had a razor and kept fairly well shaved. Would give a pretty now if I could have a picture of myself as I fetched up at Fort Macleod. I had been sixteen days, covering about 150 miles. After selling my furs and buying a saddle horse, I was not long in locating some of my companions.

When coming down from north of the Canadian line one day, I had been riding quite a circuitous route, not wanting to meet anyone of the Mounted Police. I was west of the Sweetgrass Hills when it got dark. After crossing what I took to be the Cut Bank Creek, on account of its depth below the benchlands—namely about two hundred feet and very difficult to get up or down in the dark—I rode some distance out on the benchland, unsaddled my horse, lay down in my saddle and went to sleep.

I awoke at sunrise, and laying just a few feet from me was what had been a wooden shoe box that had had several Indian children buried in it. The box had broken up; the weather and coyotes had scattered the bodies. On sitting up, I saw skeletons, pieces of blankets, skulls, and hair all around me. About a year before, the Blackfoot Indians had had the smallpox, and a great many of them had died. I was in the middle of their burying ground.

Indians sometimes travel long distances on foot and alone, either running away from some agency or going on a visit to another tribe, and they are usually hungry. One walked into my camp one evening and made me the sign for something to eat, by pointing his hand to his mouth. I had some bread on hand which had been baked on a shovel before the fire. I started to fry him elk steak in an over-sized frying pan which held anywhere from a pound and a half to two pounds. I cut the steaks thick and did the cooking while he ate. When he made the sign of enough he had eaten the bread and what had been six frying pans of meat. He slept by my fire that night and left in the morning after eating a light breakfast. "Huh, white man good medicine," was all he said.

Recently in a magazine, I saw a story of the Jackson Hole country in my old days, in which the author called our crowd the "Train Robbers Syndicate." A great many names were mentioned. I knew most of them. I met a young fellow who came into the Hole with a man named Henry Johnson. Johnson told me the young man was a Dalton, one of the boys who survived the shooting at Coffeyville, Kansas. I got to know him quite well but never knew whether he was a Dalton or not.

There was quite a lot of respect shown the boys from Jackson Hole by the soldiers in Yellowstone National Park. For instance, myself and one companion were passing through the southwest corner of the Park one day when we met two soldiers on the trail. At that time no person was allowed to carry firearms in the Park unless they were wrapped with tape and sealed, which ours were not. We had one pack horse, and out of the top of the pack stuck the shank end of a quarter of elk meat. It was summertime and out of season for killing elk.

The first question from the soldiers was: "What kind of meat is that sticking out of that pack?"

My answer was elk meat.

"Where are you boys from?"

"Jackson Hole," I replied.

"How is everything going on down there?" they asked.

"Oh, just fine," and after a few minutes more of conversation we rode on, and with their permission we stopped at their camp on Fire Hole River and got some grub such as flour, sugar, bacon, and coffee. We left them no money for we were short of funds.

When Owen Wister came into Jackson Hole one summer while writing *The Virginian,* I had several long chats with him and liked him very much. I didn't think so much of his book, though, when it came out.

Among the tales told in the presence of Owen Wister was the one about changing the babies at the dance. The incident happened over on the Rosebud River in Montana. John Huntsinger and I were living in a cabin on the Rosebud at that time. John was a practical joker.

It was generally understood that women living in isolated places too long at a time either went loco, ran off with some cowpuncher, or did something else equally bad. Their nerves did not seem to be able to stand that condition only about so long, and right now it looked as though something was about to happen. So when something would happen that gave them something to talk about or get excited over, it helped them mentally, although they never knew it. For that reason we never got any credit for the service rendered.

The baby incident happened about the holidays. Now it was spring and they needed shaking up again. Huntsinger took it upon himself to clarify the condition. Just before we were leaving for Northern Montana to represent the Bar-R outfit, Huntsinger went up one side of the Rosebud and down the other, and at almost every house he told some tale of what Bill Smith's wife had said about John James' wife, or what Tom Johnson's had said about Will Barnes's; he also spread choice bits of gossip for the younger set. Huntsinger was A-1 as a storyteller. We lost no time in leaving after Huntsinger got back to the cabin. Well, the straightening out of things never did get quite to the shooting point, but it did have the desired effect of tiding those women over to the next season.

Soon after my arrival in Montana, I bought a ranch and started in as a rancher. I made my last trip into Jackson Hole during 1900. Our Indian war had given it a great deal of advertising; the country was filled up with pilgrims and it didn't look good to me any more. There had already begun to be some talk about dude ranches.

PART III

Ranching in Montana, 1896–1905

CHAPTER THIRTEEN

I BORROW A LITTLE MONEY

THE FIRST TIME I ever borrowed money from a bank was in 1895. I had picked out the ranch I wanted to buy, together with a small bunch of cattle, and fifty head of horses. It was a cash deal and the price had been decided on. I found myself about a thousand dollars short.

Picking what I thought was the best town in the state of Montana, I entered a national bank and stepped up to the cashier's window. I told him I wanted to borrow some money. He looked at me coldly and said, "Young man, there are lots of people like you in that respect." I felt a hot flush go over my face while the cashier still looked at me with contempt.

"Isn't a bank a place where people borrow money?" I asked.

Then he spoke quite angrily: "Who are you and where do you come from?"

I told him my name.

He then looked me over carefully for a few seconds and said: "Are you *so* and *so* and *so?*"

I replied: "Yes I am."

I saw a smile go over his face as he opened the little wicker gate and stuck out his hand saying: "Crawford, I want to shake hands with you. I thought you were seven feet tall. Come in and meet the president."

It seemed as though my reputation either for good or bad had got to town ahead of me. This was shortly after the Indian war, and I guess they had heard some big stories. The president, cashier, and I spent the better part of an hour talking. I was simply answering questions. When I went away I had the desired amount of cash, and had only signed a note. The cashier and I became real friends and for quite a number of years afterward made money off each other.

The ranch was on Freeman Creek in Meagher County, Montana. The land was part of the Northern Pacific Railroad land grants. I had a survey line run in and, within a few years, what with homestead and desert claims, the railroad land I had bought, together with some government land unavoidably fenced in, my ranch greatly increased in size and value.

What I had bought for a ranch was an assignment of a homestead and desert claim, making 480 acres of land, very little of it under fence, a small cabin, poor corrals, 114 head of she-stock and 50 head of horses. It would cut about fifty tons of wild hay a year. When I sold out ten years later there were in round numbers sixteen thousand acres of land, cutting one thousand tons of hay per year, plenty of wagons, mowing machines, hay rakes, and harnesses. There were twenty miles of good fence, and about one thousand acres of land under irrigation. The hay was a mixture of timothy, blue and wild grass.

We had a good set of corrals with water in all of them, cow sheds, branding chutes, barns, and other buildings.

There were good feed grounds, four big fields or pastures cornering at the corrals, with a lane going to the outside range, all arranged in such a way that a bunch of cattle could be worked in any way you desired. I had six hundred head of she-stock.

I was a strong believer in heredity, and had stocked up with purebred Herefords and Shorthorn bulls. The sire for my saddle-horse band was General Haskell, a thorough-bred, bought when he was three years old from Dr. Blake of Helena. His pedigree went back to that wonderful horse Salvator.

At the time of selling, I had three colts from General Haskell old enough to break. They showed speed and stability. During the last winter on the ranch I rode General Haskell through the mountains in very deep snow and bitter cold weather to Helena, Montana. I was obliged to spend the night in Trout Creek Gulch with no shelter for my horse. In the morning his ears were hanging straight out to the side. However he had wonderful nerve, and I rode him the balance of the way, about twenty-two miles, and turned him over to the State Veterinary, Dr. Byrd. In two days the horse was dead from pneumonia. I was also the owner of Kitty Putnam, a famous pacer. I had bought her, about the time her racing days were over, for breeding purposes.

Concerning game on the ranch: After the haystacks were opened in winter and hauling begun from them, a great many prairie chickens would come and feed on the wild strawberries which were dried and in the hay. The chickens were never molested.

On the ranch at almost any time it would take but a few hours to go and kill blacktail deer, a bear, or a dozen blue grouse. Antelope were then getting scarce. After early snows in the fall, grasshoppers would be caught unawares. They

101

would crawl up the bunch grass, get on top of the snow, and being stiff, not able to jump. Literally thousands of blue grouse could be seen feeding on the stiff hoppers. There would also be a sprinkling of skunks walking around among them doing the same.

The late Charlie Russell, the "cowboy artist," and I were good friends. I first met Russell in the early nineties. He was living at Cascade, Montana, with Ben Roberts who ran a saddle shop.

I knew Calamity Jane well. She told me about her departure from New York City, where she had been in some kind of refuge home. Calamity had been for many years a hard drinker and could only last about so long without drinking hooch. She had been in the home about as long as she could stand it, and one day slipped out for a round of drinks. A few blocks away she got into a saloon and proceeded to "liquor up." She had got on quite a jag, when some of the attendants from the home found her. She had expected that, and in the meantime, had cached a quart of liquor somewhere in her dress. She went to her room and started in on the quart. It was not long before she started a roughhouse, which must have been lots of fun from the way she laughed while telling the story to me. After it was all over she wired Cody (Buffalo Bill) for the price of a ticket to Montana, which he sent her.

Calamity was a real wild and woolly early-day character of the West. From the time as a young girl when she was taken prisoner by a band of Indians who burned her wagon train, until she was an old lady, her life was filled with very striking events.

I knew a girl who worked for a considerable time in the dance halls of Helena, Montana, who said she was Calamity's daughter; and I believe she was. On two or three occasions we spoke of her mother. Calamity Jane had once married a ranchman in the Dakotas. In speaking of her husband, Calamity said she liked him very much but it was "just too damn quiet." She could not stay still.

For a good many years Calamity's life was about like this: She would be in a dance hall until three or four o'clock in the morning dressed in a short frock, dancing and drinking. Maybe by sunrise she would be in the saddle with a bunch of men, vigilantes, dressed in chaps and six-shooters, going to hang somebody. She made several trips with wagon trains across the plains, mainly as cook for the outfits. She had served as a soldier dressed in men's clothes on several occasions and made a full hand as cowpuncher.

I had also a speaking acquaintance with X. Beidler, an early-day character, a veteran of the old vigilante days of Virginia City, Montana. He spent a good deal of his time as shotgun messenger in and around that city.

It was always a mystery to me what became of the money that was supposed to have been made by the various characters of the early West. I mean the saloon men, tinhorn gamblers, outlaws, hurdy-gurdy girls, prospectors, cattle rustlers, and all the rest of that type. When a prospector came to town after making his stake, usually having several thousand dollars, sometimes nearly fifty thousand, he would last from ninety days to around six months, depending a good deal on what time of year it was. He left most of it with the dance-hall girls and saloons. He was not strong on gambling.

Speaking of this class of girls, they differed very little in any part of the West, from the Río Grande to British Columbia. As gold diggers, they were past grand masters and were well versed in the ways of iniquity. For instance, a prospector or mining man would drop in with a full poke of

103

dust. After a few drinks it would not be anything unusual for him to pay a girl anywhere from fifty dollars to one hundred dollars for the privilege of being her dance partner for the night. But by the middle of the night she would have her partner drunk and put to bed and be back on the floor with other partners until morning. After being cleaned he was perfectly satisfied to go back to the hills looking for more gold; he usually died broke.

Now if one of the girls died or was killed, there was a receptacle of some kind (usually a bowl) set on one of the dance-hall tables for contributions to meet the funeral expenses. I have seen outlaws killed, and someone would pass the hat before the grave-digging would start. This procedure also held good for tinhorn gamblers. When a camp would blow up, everybody was broke, and the saloon man arriving at a new camp would have to make a touch in order to open up again. The girls would all be in debt to the landlady, who was also doing business on borrowed money. What money she made she either gave it to her tinhorn friend or it was stolen from her by him, who in turn passed it on to his lady friend, who in turn ran away with some slim-waisted, long-backed cowpuncher. But as a matrimonial venture it never lasted very long. When some lucky prospector had saved up a stake for a little girl he had left back in the home town, and tried to get out with it by rolling it in his blankets and getting on a stagecoach, some bandit would hold up the stage and take it away from him.

Yet someone passed the hat to bury all the bandits I ever knew, when they cashed in. I guess the fellow back in Kentucky who sold the liquor got all the money or, on second thought, I don't believe that is right either, for most of the whisky was made out of creek water and something that the drugstore sent in.

CHAPTER FOURTEEN

MONTANA HORSES AND COWBOYS

I THINK THE MONTANA CAYUSE was the best cow horse I ever knew. He was a cross between the old Spanish mares of California and some thoroughbred studs brought from Kentucky, and weighed from 850 to 950 pounds. He could buck harder, jump higher, last longer, and run faster than any other horse north of the Río Grande. I have seen cowpunchers from Texas, who came to Montana with a shipment of cattle, after being bucked off until they were perfectly satisfied, sit down and cry. Most all of them finally drifted back south, where they rode small mustang horses.

Montana men brought the thoroughbred studs from Kentucky for racing purposes. Their colts, when being tried out as two-year-olds, had to make the time that would bring home the bacon or they were turned loose on the range. This method developed a horse, not a pony. I have, on several occasions, ridden the same horse one hundred actual miles between sun and sun. He was a beauty to look at, with short, stout back, flat legs, small ears, lots of savvy; and he seemed to know how to take care of himself. The

Montana range grass, I always thought, from spring up to about August, was equal in strength to feeding grain.

The cowpunchers whom I met in the south as a boy differed greatly from the ones I got acquainted with and knew in later years in the north. The bunch I knew in the south were mostly holdovers from the old trailherds of the seventies. They had followed the herds on the Chisholm Trail, to Caldwell, Wichita, Abilene, then taken the Blember Trail to Dodge City and Hays City. To begin with, a majority of them had been getaway men and roughnecks from the Eastern cities. They never knew much about a cow, but after getting to be fairly good shots with a .45 they became bad men and would shoot with very little provocation, especially if they had a little advantage. They were not a long-lived race of men. They were not long in meeting some fellows who knew what the old cow was saying to her calf. The early settlers of Montana sprang from a race of people who came west during the gold rush of the sixties. A majority of them came from the Southern states. They generally entered into legitimate business, became miners, prospectors, ranchers, merchants, stage drivers, bullwhackers, or any other thing that had to be done to build up a new country. Their children were about the big-boy size when Montana began to grow cattle. These boys literally grew up in the saddle, and knew about an old cow and a cayuse.

The Montana cowboy was not so quick to pull his gun as the Texan; however he was just as good a shot. When he did draw he was quicker in many cases than the man from the south. Nearly all first-class cowpunchers could keep a tin can rolling with a six-shooter in one hand and roll a cigarette with the other.

The advent of the Northern Pacific and Great Northern railroads brought their quota of thugs from the eastern cities.

From their ranks came a good many of the tinhorn gamblers and all-round bad men who were responsible for most of the killings.

Cowpunchers as a rule played a reasonable, good and fair game of cards, especially when around the camp. But when they were in town with a few drinks under their belts, they were pretty easy picking for tinhorn gamblers. However, the tinhorns did not always win. I saw a game of poker one night in a saloon in a small town on the Great Northern. When the lights were relit there were four dead men on the floor; three of them tinhorn gamblers.

One time in the month of November, when the water in the Missouri River was just about as cold as ice, we tried to ford a small bunch of wild beef steers. We held them up against the water for two or three hours, trying to make them take to the river. They would not go in, and we were doing a good deal of harm to the beef. So we decided to go to a ferry which was a few miles from there, where a fence wing had been built out on both sides of the road from the landing for the purpose of loading livestock. The boat was fifty or sixty feet long and about fourteen feet wide.

We had considerable trouble getting them to take the boat but finally, getting about half of them on, we started across. There was one two-by-four scantling across the front end of the boat, about three feet high. My position was sitting on my horse, crossways of the boat, up against this scantling. The ferry man had been given a horse to ride and was told to steer the boat without getting off of his horse, as the cattle were wild and not accustomed to seeing a man on foot. The cattle seemed tame enough, being tired from all day handling.

The ferryboat was pulling across the river with the current. We got midstream; the cattle were very quiet. To the

107

ferryman, they seemed gentle enough so he quietly eased off of his horse. He could more easily handle the boat on foot. I have seen entire herds of cattle leave the bed ground in the twinkling of an eye. Well, it was just like that. I only heard a swish; my horse was struck broadside by about half the cattle; overboard we went with them—all the cattle on top of us.

I had on winter clothing, a pair of chaps and six gun, with a beltful of cartridges. The horse was on top of me, and the cattle on top of him. I have never been so deep under water in my life as I was then, and hitting me all over were legs and horns. I thought I would never come to the top. I was a good swimmer and worked hard to come up. When I did come up I was about fifty feet below the boat, the river running swift. There were cattle all around me, but my horse was a long way off. I had about got my breath, when a steer came up right alongside of me. I grabbed him by the horn. His back was low under water, and I got aboard and caught him with my spurs. He let out a big bawl. We were headed for the right side of the river so I kept him steered in that direction. I was badly strangled and very cold. I don't think I could have gotten out without help.

We came up about fifty yards below the landing. When near the other side I slipped off behind my steer, held on to his tail, and let go just as he was getting out.

The cattle which were being held on the bank saw the others in the water and all came in and swam across. I held onto some bushes with just my head out of water until the entire bunch had got out. One of the boys brought me my horse, and in a few minutes my clothes were frozen stiff, which kept me from getting very cold. The steers had gone down the road on a fast trot, and we were not long in getting somewhere.

Among the cowboy's duties as line rider was holding the cattle back and not letting them drift too far during storms, keeping them on good feed, and getting them out of dangerous places. The Missouri River was a very dangerous stream. Cattle, in large droves, would collect in the river bottom. Before the ice would entirely close the river there would be long open places near the center. Cattle, after several days of thirst and especially if the sun would shine for a while, would, by milling, hooking, and pushing, work out onto the ice, trying to get to the open water. The ice usually broke and let the whole bunch in. They would go under the ice and all be lost.

Line riders would locate a place where the ice was solid clear across and, by dragging dirt out on it in a dry cowhide from the horn of the saddle, would make a trail across the river and get the cattle started single file. In that way they would save a great many cattle from drowning. It was very difficult to get dirt as the ground would be frozen as hard as rock. If wood was plentiful we would build a fire to thaw out the dirt. I have read stories where it was said the cattle pawed for feed in the snow. Horses and sheep paw the snow for feed, but cattle only root with their noses.

The roundup chuck wagon was usually pulled by four horses. At the start in the spring, usually two or three of the horses were only half broken. In crossing creeks, there were no bridges. If the team was dry the driver would have to throw the whip into the leaders and not let them stop until the wheelers were in the water. Otherwise the wheelers would step over the lead bars and the wagon tongue would poke into the leaders. In a fraction of a second everyone of

109

the team would be bucking, kicking, and going out of the water on a dead run, which usually wound up in a wreck and a late dinner. The Montana cayuse is gentle enough until something goes wrong; then he is a whirlwind.

When swimming a saddle horse with a double-cinch rig on him, it is best to loosen your hind cinch, as a horse uses lots of wind when he has very far to swim; also, he can't blow himself up with a tight hind cinch. I have seen a horse, after becoming very tired from being compelled to swim a long time, straightening out cattle, fill himself with air, turn up on his side and float downstream presumably until he was rested, then get back on his stomach and swim ashore.

I was making a forced ride in Montana, late in November one year, when about the middle of the afternoon I was struck by a severe blizzard which fairly howled and blew about forty miles an hour—a real gale. There was such snow and frost that I could scarcely breathe, and the temperature was at least twenty degrees below zero. Besides my ordinary clothes, I had only a slicker. Up to that time the weather had been fairly warm. I faced the storm for about half an hour. There was a good chance of getting lost and freezing, as it was all open country. It was very difficult to make my horse face the storm, and I was about ready to give up and let him turn around when I fetched up in a canyon which I had been making for. It had rock sides from fifty to one hundred feet high, and was very narrow, with a creek running through it. The creek was ordinarily about knee deep, and about twenty or thirty feet wide. It was one of those creeks that freeze on the bottom first and was now swollen to about three feet deep, jammed with snow and slush ice. The boulders in the bottom were covered with ice, making them very slippery.

To go down the canyon I would have had to cross the

creek about every fifty yards. Even if my horse had not fallen down, we soon would have been wet all over and have probably frozen to death. There was a good deal of wood on the hillside at a break in the rocks and it was fairly well protected, so I stopped there to spend the night. I had on only buckskin gloves, and my hands were so numb I could scarcely use them. In trying to light a fire, my matches got into the snow and would not burn. It looked for a time as though I would freeze to death anyway. I had no food or blankets, and was afraid to unsaddle my horse because he had been ridden hard and I knew he would freeze. I finally cut open the shoulder of my coat, got out a small handful of cotton padding and shot into the edge of it with a .45. This started it to burn while I held it among some pitch-pine splinters on the ground, and finally fanned it into a blaze. The blizzard broke about the middle of the next day and I rode out of there; I had not spent a very pleasant night.

I have had my gun "freeze up" during cold rides, so that the first shot would scarcely go out of the barrel. It would take several shots before the gun would act anyway normal. I have also had a quart bottle of whisky freeze nearly solid in the pocket of my buffalo overcoat.

One winter I came in from the roundup with my string of saddle horses, and when I reached the ranch of an old friend, Jake Hammon, I found him sick, without medicine, and not a soul there to take care of him. My horses were already turned loose, they had begun to scatter, and it was dark. I could not make a start for medicine until morning.

I started on a 100-mile trip for medicine early the next morning. Halfway I left my horse at Fort Logan where I took a fresh one loaned to me by a friend. From the Fort I went to White Sulphur Springs, got the medicine, a quart

111

of whisky, and rode back there, returning the horse to my friend. Riding my own horse, I reached the starting point of the morning, having ridden 110 miles between sunrise and dark. The days were very short. Though the whisky was put in the pocket of a buffalo overcoat, it was frozen when I got to the old man's ranch. I stayed with him about two weeks and then went on about my business.

My horse that made half that hard day's trip was named "Johnnie." One day a sheriff came to my ranch and told me that he was looking for a man who had made a getaway from Minnesota eighteen years before. He described my cook, John Smith, whom I liked and who had been an old roundup cook. After the officer had left, I went to the cook's sleeping quarters and told him about it.

"Yes," he said, "I am the man he wants."

I asked what he was wanted for.

He said: "I shot my wife when I found her in bed with another man."

"Do you want to go or wait and let him take you?"

"No, I don't want him to take me anywhere."

I gave him what money I had on me, and told him to go to the barn and saddle old Johnnie, which he did and left. That was the last of Johnnie; I never saw him again. I guess they rode out of the country. I never heard of his being arrested.

You occasionally see strange mirages on the Plains. A man who was not accustomed to riding on the range left the ranch house with me one morning. We were riding down a dim road through a meadow where the grass had been mowed. There were about eight inches of new snow on the ground, and a little fog in the air. We saw what my friend took to be two men on horseback, riding toward us side by side. I told him to keep his eye on them. When we came up

112

to them, they turned out to be two thistle stalks, standing about one foot apart and sticking up about six inches above the snow.

The worst blizzard I ever saw or went through was in Montana. I was camped at an elevation of about six or seven thousand feet and saw that howling, blowing, snowing blizzard last for seventeen days and nights.

It came early in the winter season, and for that reason not much range stock was lost. There was a mountain side near by which was covered with thick fir timber. The cattle began to go into the timber about the middle of the afternoon before the blizzard struck, and kept coming and going into it all night long, keeping up a constant mooing. None of the cattle came out of there during the seventeen days that the storm lasted. When the storm was over, and the cattle were all out, I went into their bed ground in the timber. There was a spot about one acre in extent where they had stood and milled around in a tight bunch. They came out single file making a deep trench, their backs just showing above the snow. Nearly five feet of snow fell during the storm; it was tramped and packed solid, making a snow corral. There were no dead ones out of the bunch, which I estimated to number about a thousand head. They certainly smelled the blizzard coming about eighteen hours before it got there, and got ready for it.

The warm wind, called the "chinook," does not feel warm. It generally feels raw and chilly. For example, it will start to blow just before dark, when the ground is covered with a cold, frosty, crusted snow, anywhere from a foot to three feet in depth, and will continue to blow a gale all night. When morning comes the entire landscape is a brown to black color. Nearly every vestige of snow is gone, leaving a white patch here and there. All coulees are running over with muddy water. Sometimes it turns to zero weather while the ground is still soppy with water. Then the range gets covered with ice, and the livestock suffer. I have seen soft wet snow and running water on the mountains, while in the valley, a thousand feet lower down, there would be a temperature of twenty degrees below zero. I have also seen just the reverse; bitter cold on the mountains and warm in the valleys. One time I was in the Prickly Pear Valley, five miles north of Helena, Montana, when the temperature was forty below zero. I could hear people in Helena talking and the clang of the streetcars very plainly.

One time a companion and I were crossing through the Clarks Fork country in northern Wyoming, just east of Yellowstone Park, on a long, hard ride. My horse, in particular, had been ridden hard and far, and his feet were worn down to the quick. With every rod we made he grew slower, and his lameness became worse; it is very disagreeable to ride a tender-footed horse.

We saw some thirty head of horses that had started to trail down to water, and upon looking them over, but without exciting them, we saw there were several saddle horses in the bunch. One of them showed the earmarks of having some hot blood in him, and that was the one I wanted. I got down to the water ahead of the bunch. It was a small brushy creek with some rimrocks on the opposite side, where the horses would have to go through. To throw my rope was difficult since I had to get close to the brush on the upside so as not to be seen. There was no place to maneuver so I tied my rope fast to the saddle.

My partner had been holding them back as much as he could, but they hit the branch on the run. I spotted the one I wanted, but he was pretty well out on the far side of the bunch, with his head high. I pitched my rope on him and

114

when he came to the end of it, and the rope tautened up, three more horses jumped against it. My horse was jerked down flat; the horse that I had caught was facing me and was sitting back on the rope. I looked for something to break before the loose horses got untangled and got away, but everything held.

We led the caught horse across the creek and up onto the little bench which was fairly level but rocky. I turned my lame horse loose, and he walked away about a hundred yards and stood there. I don't think the new horse moved a foot while I was saddling him but when I stepped across him, he went after me pretty lively, using what is called the "sunfish" style. He would jump to first one side and then the other, and nearly change ends while in the air. He would hit the ground all spread out, with all legs stiff, giving me about four different jolts at the same time. I was riding him all right until I heard a pistol shot, and my horse began to fold up and lie down. My partner sat on his horse, near by, laughing.

"What did you shoot him for?" I asked with some amazement.

"The hell I shot him! You shot him yourself."

He had bucked my six-shooter out of the open scabbard. The hammer had been resting on a loaded shell, which was not very often the case, and the gun went off. The horse was shot through the stomach. There was nothing to do now but get my crippled horse and ride away.

At sunrise next morning I changed horses. We met a boy who was hitching up to a plow in an old stubble field. I gave him a smile, saying "Good morning son, we are going to trade horses. Of course you don't know it but we are." I proceeded to unsaddle my horse, unhitch his horse from the plow, put my saddle on him, and ride away. The boy would

115

have a much better horse than I after a little rest and feeding, but I was willing to give him the best of the bargain. I had need of a horse with good feet right at that time. If that boy should ever read this, he will know who it was that he got the best of in that horse trade.

Quite often, while riding through the country, a freight outfit would be met up with. Freight outfits usually had three wagons with from twelve to fifteen tons of freight, and carried liquor in barrels. Now if the bunch of boys who met the freighter wanted a drink, a barrel would be rolled out on the ground, and rocks placed under each end, raising the middle of the barrel about ten or twelve inches off the ground. Then a light chain, which would be taken from the team, was wrapped around the center of the barrel and twisted up with a crowbar. The liquor would come out of all the seams and into a dishpan underneath it. When the chain was released the staves would all tighten up again, and there wouldn't be a leak. This was called "sweating" a barrel of liquor. The freighter and his swampers were sometimes a little sore but would usually wind up by taking a drink too, then feeling better, and treating the matter lightly.

I blew into Livingston, Montana, one cold day in the month of April. I say "blew in," and I litterly was. The Indians called that country the "home of the winds." It was making good that day by blowing a gale which would toss pebbles from the street into my face.

I had spent some time in an Indian camp and was loaded up with graybacks. Soldiers call them "cooties." I only had the horse I was riding, no change of clothes and no money. The cooties were making it so lively for me that I couldn't stand it any longer. I crossed the Yellowstone River and turned upstream a short distance to a vacant hobo camp.

I found an empty five-gallon can, built a fire, and put water on to boil. About the time the water was near boiling I took off my clothes and put them in the can. I mean *all* my clothes, even to my socks. I held my boots over the fire in the flame.

I had got my clothes pretty well dried out around the fire on the bushes near by, when an extra twist of the wind picked up my shirt and landed it in the river about fifty feet from the shore. The river was up, ice cold, and running like a mill race. I just had to have that shirt. I went in after it without a moment's hesitation, but it sank just before I reached it. Well, I found it with my feet by treading water. I landed about 150 yards below, as red as a lobster and as cold as a tin shop; but when I left that camp I was free of graybacks, and hadn't a care in the world.

CHAPTER FIFTEEN

MONTANA ROUNDUPS

THE ROUNDUP OF THE NORTH differed greatly from the roundup of the south. The south was great on trailing cattle, close herding, line riding; and usually the branding was done in corrals. Line riders were the men who rode in the neighborhood of boundary lines designated by mountain ranges, rivers, creeks, or valleys, and would turn the cattle back on what was known as their own range. On a fair sized cow outfit some of the range boundaries might be as far as one hundred miles from the home ranch. There would be small adobe or stone shacks or dugouts strung around at advantageous places on the range where the boys could camp. Many provisions from a store were not necessary as these cowpunchers were meat eaters.

The north was wide-open range. A roundup usually carried about twenty or thirty riders, each with a string of thirteen horses, i.e., thirteen horses were considered a full string. Also there would be wranglers, cooks, and two or three wagons. The roundup had a secretary and captain, and went across country paying no attention to roads. In the spring, about May 20, the calf roundup started. It covered a wide territory, making a roundup nearly every day, usually going to a new camp for the next day's work.

Each rider rode two and sometimes three horses a day. Afternoons, after the circle had been ridden, the calves were all branded and turned back with their mothers, toward the way from which they had come. They would brand from two to four hundred calves each day. The calves were roped and brought to the fire from the horn of a saddle. The rider called out the brand and earmarks of the mother; namely Bar-R, Two Dot, Three-C, Diamond-O, Bar-Ox-Bar, U-V, or whatever it might be. Men on foot, at the fire, did the branding and earmarking. The secretary kept a record of all the brands and earmarks and all calves branded. Wages were forty dollars a month, and if you furnished your own horses your pay was more.

Riding circle was the main roundup work. It was the captain's job in the morning to start the men out. You caught your horse as soon as it was light enough to see. The horse wrangler would bring the saddle-horse band into a rope corral, which was made by tying one end of a rope to a wagon wheel or tongue and holding the other end of two ropes tied together, making it about one hundred feet with a man in about the middle.

You got your orders from the captain about like: "John, you, Pete, Tom, and Curley, work the foothills from Elk Creek along west to Beaver Creek. Throw everything down out of there, and we will round up on Beaver Flats." They would work on the south side of the Flats. Jack, Jim, and Joe would be sent to work at a similar territory north of the Flats. Others would be sent west of the Flats, say Rock Creek, and would work back. Still others would work the valley on both sides and pick up a good many of the cattle that would be run out of the high mountains by the first-

119

named riders. You would all get to the Flats about the same time, namely about the middle of the afternoon. The cook with a helper would bring up the wagons; the horse wrangler would bring up the saddle horses. You would bring the herd within about a mile of camp then leave a couple of men with them and all go in to eat dinner and get a change of horses.

During the spring roundup in Meagher County, Montana, I had left camp about sunrise with one companion called Skeeter, with instructions to ride Jim Ball Basin. Jim Ball Basin lies between the Missouri and Smith rivers about fifty miles in a northeasterly direction from Helena. We were to bring down all cows and calves. It was about the first of June and not many she-stock had got up into that high country yet. The north sides of banks and coulees were still black with matted-down weeds where the snow had only been gone a short while. The flats and ridges were well up in green grass with a sprinkle of wild flowers. Jim Ball Basin was a high plateau; the surface was fairly level with patches of white-pine timber about lodgepole size. Lodgepoles are white-pine poles about three inches through at the big end and twelve to sixteen feet long. They are cut and peeled by the Indians for tipis or lodges. When dry they are light and strong.

Jim Ball Basin also had low ridges, some scattered fir trees and small bunches of rocks, and an area of several miles each way. You could ride a horse down out of there in most any direction, although the basin was about on a level with the top of the Belt Range. It was what was called "high country."

Skeeter and I had separated, and I was coming up a small rise when my horse began to whistle. I was not surprised at this for you can always expect something when riding high country; I mean a band of deer, elk, a bear, or wolves. Now one thing that will nearly always make a horse whistle is a bear.

When I got to the top of the little ridge my horse began to cut up some, for about one hundred feet from me stood a big roachback bear with two cubs playing on the ground. She had been tearing open rotten logs and turning over stones looking for bugs and worms. The little cubs were hunting with her like biddies with a hen.

My horse got the bit in his teeth and went off sideways with me for probably seventy-five or one hundred yards before I could get the bit away from him and get him stopped. I then worked him back up to within fifty or seventy feet of the bear, who by this time had started to go to a patch of lodgepole timber. She was slapping the cubs ahead of her. They were only about the size of a house cat and didn't want to go.

She raised on her hind feet and danced around plenty. She had a mane down the back of her neck to her shoulders about eight inches long and acted pretty mad. My horse was still whistling and trying to stampede. There was a small fir tree close by with limbs about eight or ten feet from the ground. I guess the old bear thought she had to fight me. She pushed the cubs over to the tree, then slapped them and boosted them up the tree. She then came walking out to meet me. I had had about enough fun by this time, so rode away and left her. She put her front feet on a log and watched me out of sight.

When Skeeter and I met, I saw that he had not heard any of the noise we made so I said nothing to him about it. Nor did I say anything to the boys in camp about it for several days, until we had moved out of that district. There are always some of the cowboys who will shoot up a bear whenever they meet one, and I didn't want the old mother bear to be disturbed.

Nearly all roundups carried a "twister." He rode a string of broncos (horses that were being broken to ride), and would haze your horse in the morning for a few minutes, if you didn't feel like getting ginned up before riding out on the circle.

Cowboys who had cattle on the range and rode in the roundup would get their own calves branded and beef gathered and have some money from the roundup besides. After the calves were branded, the roundup turned back and gathered beef. The mavericks were usually sold to someone working with the outfit at about ten dollars each. A "maverick" is a calf with no brand on him already weaned from the mother—one that was missed in the spring or fall roundup. All bummers found were eaten. A "bummer" is an unweaned calf, about a yearling or more, which has two or three different cows that he can make stand still until he gets all their milk. His nose is always slick and shiny, and he is rolling fat and tender.

There was usually time enough between the calf and the beef roundups for the boys to pitch a small party, and they usually did. Also they lost no time in having a party at the end of the season, which lasted about eight months. At this time the expenses were figured up. Calves branded and beef gathered ran about one dollar a head.

Cowpunchers were usually a reckless set, tenderhearted, and bashful around the women. Most of them had a song or two that they would sing. Some of them sang very well. I always thought an old cow handled better when she had someone to sing to her.

The old-timers drew the line at ranch work, but if left there in winter to look after the weaned calves and early

122

heifers, they were absolutely dependable. Nearly all ranches had one or two around during the winter, and it was necessary, sometimes, toward spring for some old-timer to "ride grub line." That is, he would go from one ranch to another and stay a few days at each. He was always welcome, and if you wanted a horse broken to ride he would ride him. He spent most of his time making quirts and rawhide ropes. Winter horses around the ranch were called "diggers." They were old roundup horses, stiff in the shoulders, or not good enough for the hard work that circle riding demanded.

Rawhide ropes were made about like this: Take a green hide, i.e., one just removed from a beef, stake it out flat on the ground, and leave it there until it is about half-dry. If the hide is an old dry one, the best way is to throw it into running water, and in a few days it will be as soft as a wet rag and you can usually slip the hair off. Then stretch it out on the ground the same as the green hide.

Start in the center by first cutting out an oblong piece about two inches wide and about eight or ten inches long. Begin at the edge of the hole to cut a strip about one half inch wide. Cut around from the center until the entire hide is one long strip like a carpet rag. Now cut it into four pieces of equal length. If you haven't time to go ahead with it, but must wait for stormy weather, wrap it up in a wet burlap or something that will keep it damp. The next thing is to take a sharp knife and shave the hair off. If the rope you are making is to be used on the home range, just around the corrals, you may leave the hair on and it will soon wear off. Now on a table fix a sizer made out of an old razor or drawshave. Stretch the strands well while they are damp. Pull the strands through the sizer the flat way, in order to make them all the same thickness, and stretch them again.

123

Fix another sizer by placing some sharp blade upright in a table or board and driving a nail the distance from the blade that you want the strands to be in width. After pulling your strands through this sizer they should be all of equal width and thickness.

Wrap the strands into four balls, always keeping them damp. Fasten the ends and braid a four-strand square braid, always taking considerable pains with the braiding. When the braiding is done the rope will be square. Lay it on the floor, put a small short board on it, and roll it back and forth with your foot. It will soon become perfectly round and smooth. By frequent oiling with tallow or vegetable fat, your rope will soon become shiny and nearly black.

A good rawhide rope is a joy to any cowpuncher's heart. It gets better with age, is very strong, and if not handled too roughly, will last for many years. The advantage over a grass rope is in the weight, especially in throwing from a running horse in the wind, also in that it will give and stretch. A forty-five-foot rawhide rope, when put onto a heavy animal, will stretch four to six feet. This makes it easy on the horse as well as on the animal being caught.

It was customary, in most parts of the cow country, especially in the north, after the beef roundup or during the holidays, for the boys and girls to get together and go on a regular dance spree. They would all go from one ranch to another, taking the music with them, and dance nearly every night. Some of the dancers would drop out and some more would be picked up on the way. The circle would take from ten days to two weeks.

Some of the dance calls were quite amusing, for instance: "Hit the lumber with your leather," "Steers in the center and cows all round," "Swing Grandma," "Now rope and balance all," "Stampede you know where." Other calls were made up from the different districts such as "The Big Horn Boys and the Sweetwater Girls." Other districts such as "Stinking Water" and "Big Hole" all came in for their share.

There was sometimes sung as these dances a song known as the "Cowboy's Christmas Ball." It was very much of a favorite and had the calls of several square dances in it. Some of these figures were used at nearly all the dances and went about like this when Bill commenced to holler:

Now fellows shake your pen. Lock horns ter all them heifers and rustle them like men. Salute yer lovely critters. Now swing and let 'em go. Climb the grapevine round them, now all hands do-see-do. You mavericks join the roundup; just skip the waterfall. All pull your freight together; now swallow fork and change. Big Boston lead the trail herd, through little Pitchfork range. Purr round yer gentle pussies, now rope and balance all.

The dance usually closed by everybody's singing and dancing a song called "Old Paint" which took the place of "Home Sweet Home." It was sung to waltz music:

Good-by, Old Paint, I'm leaving Cheyenne,
Good-by, Old Paint, I'm leaving Cheyenne.

My foot in the stirrup my pony won't stand,
Good-by, Old Paint, I'm leaving Cheyenne.

I'm leaving Cheyenne, I'm off for Montan',
Good-by, Old Paint, I'm leaving Cheyenne.
I'm riding Old Paint, I'm leading Old Fan,
Good-by, Old Paint, I'm leaving Cheyenne.

With my feet in the stirrup my bridle in my hand,
Good-by, Old Paint, I'm leaving Cheyenne.

125

Old Paint's a good pony, he paces when he can,
Good-by, Little Annie, I'm off for Montan'.

The music usually shut off soon after the dance started, and the dancers furnished the music by singing and shuffling with their feet. There were several more verses to "Old Paint," but this will give you an idea of the breaking up of a ball. After that you would get a few hours' sleep on the floor or maybe in the hay, until breakfast was ready, then leave about the middle of the afternoon for the next location. The words and tune of "Old Paint" would still be going around in my head for a long time after the dance season was over. The spree usually wound up with one or two weddings.

CHAPTER SIXTEEN

THE STRANGE WAYS OF BAD MEN

A BAD MAN will sometimes lose his nerve. One afternoon I rode into a small town in Montana. One street was about all there was of it. I had hardly gotten my horse to a hitching rail when an acquaintance informed me that Flat Nose George was in town. He had been looking for me, arguing very freely about a little grievance he had against me, and said he would kill me on sight. I stepped into a saloon and drank a small beer, talked a few minutes and went out. I didn't want any trouble with Flat Nose, but I couldn't have any peace of mind until it was over, no matter how it ended. I started the round of saloons looking for him. The atmosphere had begun to grow tense, and there were few people on the street. Now and then I could see a man backed up into some doorway, just standing there. One or two barkeepers said, "Yes, Flat Nose was here a few minutes ago but has just stepped out."

At the end of the street there was a livery stable. The hostler of the stable was standing in front of the stable and motioned to me with his thumb. I took it to mean that Flat Nose was in there. The barn door was standing open. Inside there were double stalls along both sides. The middle was open with a dirt floor. When I stepped inside I pulled my gun. I thought that might be the best thing to do to avoid trouble. When I reached the middle of the barn. I stepped into an empty stall which had the manger full of hay—in fact it looked too full. I looked at the hostler, and he motioned again with his thumb, which I understood to mean that he was there. I stepped up to the manger and poked the barrel of my gun down into the hay. It struck Flat Nose in the ribs. I made him get out, took his gun, emptied out the shells, gave it back to him and told him to leave town, which he did.

Flat Nose was not a coward for I had seen him tried out when we were friendly, but he was a rascal. It seems that there was a fellow sentenced to be hung in one of the Western states. Flat Nose told me that it was he who had done the killing for which the fellow was to be hung, but that the fellow needed hanging anyway so he was not going to interfere. And he didn't.

This time Flat Nose had been drinking too much liquor while in town and for the time being had completely lost his nerve. Liquor sometimes seems to have such a reaction. He was a big rough fellow, who always, winter or summer, wore his shirt open all the way down the front. He had about as much hair on his chest as a bear. I met him several times afterward but never had any trouble with him. He was later shot to death in Utah.

Bullets sometimes do freakish things. This pistol shot started a nickname for a notorius character later known as "Toothless Frank." Frank was sitting on a crosstie which answered for a step at the front entrance of a saloon in Boulder, Montana. He was a bad actor, frequently causing trouble around the dance halls and saloons. He was as tough a looking fellow as you would ever want to see or meet. His .45 hung extra low on his hip.

While he was sitting as mentioned above, rather groggy with a hangover from the night before, a lone man came riding slowly down the street. He stopped in front of Frank, pulled a .45, and shot him square in the mouth, the bullet coming out the back of his neck. I helped carry Frank into the saloon where we washed and dressed his wound. After spitting out two or three teeth, we poured a good amount of whisky down his throat, then tied up his jaw (which seemed to be loose), by putting a bandage under his chin and over the top of his head. That same night Toothless was in evidence in the saloons. He would put his hand under his chin, slip the bandage off of his head, let his jaw drop down, and take a drink. In a very short time he was as all right as he ever was.

The fellow that did the shooting rode on out of town, and no one followed him. Later on this same Toothless Frank came to my room one night at the Windsor Hotel in Boulder, and woke me up. He was hard pressed and had to make a getaway. I had two saddle horses in Hack Conconon's livery stable. I gave him a note to Hack telling him which horse to let Toothless have. At the barn, they rigged him up with an old saddle. I don't remember ever seenig Toothless again. I know I never saw the horse again.

While passing through northern Montana, I learned that an old friend of mine, named Turner, was running a saloon in Chinook, called the Barrel House. I decided to drop by and say "hello." About two years prior to this time I had been a witness for the state against some cattle thieves who had operated on Elk Creek. My evidence had caused a conviction for some of the gang. They didn't seem to like it. Information had reached me that the rest of the gang intended at some time to cook my heart and eat it. I had not met any of them since that time. I dropped my bridle reins over a hitching rail in front of the Barrel House and walked in. The room was only about twelve feet wide at the entrance. At the left was a showcase for cigars and tobacco, next about four barrels of liquor were piled up, then there was a long counter in front of the bar. Behind the bar was a long looking glass. On the opposite side of the room, that is on the right side, there was an offset which widened the room out for a pool and billiard hall. There were quite a few fellows playing pool and billiards, and Turner was in the far end of the room which was something like seventy or eighty feet long, looking after the games.

When I had gotten about even with the offset in the room and was looking in the glass behind the bar, I saw a man sitting on a bench against the wall give a quick start and at once recognized him as one of the men in the cattle deal. I didn't turn my head but he saw that I was watching him in the glass. He got up and came sidling slowly toward the bar with both arms held out like the wings of a setting hen; when he reached the bar, he laid both elbows on it. He did not want me to make any mistake about his movements. We partly patched up our trouble before I left. Anyway, we never had any further trouble.

Along in 1901 or '02, while I was on the ranch, the Kid Curry gang robbed a Great Northern train near Wagner, Montana, securing about ninety thousand dollars in unsigned bills. For a time they made a clean getaway. I was busy making hay on the ranch and on a Sunday evening was sitting in front of the bunkhouse with my old Jackson Hole companion, Skeeter. He saw a man coming riding over the hill leading a little bean-belly pack horse. We watched him as he came up, and by the time he got to us we saw that the whole thing was phony but said nothing.

His pack looked about like a cheap peddler's outfit. He said he was looking for work. I told him he was hired, to take off his pack, put it in the bunkhouse, and turn his horse in the pasture. By the time he had unpacked we knew all about his story without hearing it. It was probably the first pack horse he had ever had anything to do with. His hands didn't look like ranch hands, and he handled his gun as though he was afraid of it.

I put him to driving a rake the next morning; the following Sunday morning one of the hay hands came and told me that Mike (that is what we called him) was in the pasture field measuring the shoe tracks of my top saddle horse, Spokane. Spokane was a thoroughbred horse and I usually kept him shod in front. I told the fellow to forget it. I was running three wagons, two rakes, and three machines, most of the time cutting wild hay. There was one old man driving one machine who couldn't grind his sickle, and I usually did the grinding for him.

On a certain Saturday morning the detective had been working for me two weeks. While grinding the old man's sickle in front of the cabin, I kept looking down the creek, over the top of the barn and sheds and corrals, to the road which came up on the benchlands. The wagons and rakes were working below the house, while the machines were cutting farther up the creek above the house. I had noticed the wagons and one rake go out. I hadn't thought much about Mike, as he usually was the last one to get started out to work. It was customary for the men, when catching their horses in the round corral in the morning, to tie my horse team in the barn for me. I sometimes drove a rake and sometimes a machine or filled in most any place.

After getting the old man out to work, I went to the barn to get out my team, a pair of big white horses. They stood together in a double stall, and the harness was on pegs in the side of the barn behind them. I took down a collar which opened at the top of the neck and walked into the stall and was putting it on one of the horses when I heard a six-shooter click behind me. A very gruff voice was saying: "Put them up. Don't make any fuss about it and no false moves, the jig is all up with you."

There was quite a lot more of that kind of stuff said.

I said to him: "What is the big idea? Let me put this collar up." I had the collar in both hands holding it over my head.

He backed away toward the door through which I had come in, and I backed out from between the horses. There was another door which opened into the corral. Just beside the peg which my harness hung on was another peg which had lots of broken harness hanging on it. About the middle of the bunch of broken harness hung a .45 six-shooter in an open scabbard. I thought I would try one little dodge on him anyway, and as I hung up the collar I pretended to stumble and fell against the harness. As I did so I looked past him and motioned a little excitedly with one hand saying: "Don't shoot, Skeeter. It is only a josh." Mike fell for it and quickly whirled around; then I yelled to him to drop his gun or I would kill him. He dropped it and looking down my gun he was about the most surprised man I have ever seen. I had just backed him out of the barn when Skeeter came walking along the side of a cowshed with a .30–30 Winchester across his arm. He had been inside the cowshed watching the play all the time.

Mike had been standing just outside the door of the barn

132

which went into the corral, waiting for me. We gave the fellow a pleasant half-hour and let him go with the understanding that there would be nothing said about it as the evidence was not sufficient. I didn't think it right for him to take pay from me and from someone else at the same time. I watched him saddle and pack his little bean-belly horse and ride away.

My top saddle horse, Spokane, was stolen early that fall with several other horses from that range and were started north through Saskatchewan for the overland route to Alaska. Spokane was a sorrel horse, with two white feet and a pink ship on his nose, branded Cross Key, and vented; he was a thoroughbred and a mile race horse. He was as good a cow horse as I have ever seen or been on.

The horses were not missed from the range for several days, and we got a late start in following them. After we got the trail straightened out we made good time and were close to the thieves. A short distance north of the Saskatchewan River and six or seven hundred miles from home they learned of our coming and scattered, also scattering the horses.

The days were getting short up there, and it was a long way back on tired horses. We spent a couple of days picking up horses, and I think we brought back fourteen head—there were five men in our party. But we did not find Spokane. However, we left his description and brands with all the ranchers in that country. The following summer I received a letter from a farmer in that country telling me that a sorrel "Cross Key" horse had died that winter in a lane. That was a wheat district and all fenced up with wire. The horse thieves had undoubtedly found out what a good horse he was and had ridden him hard. He was trying to get back home when he got up against barbwire and starved.

Early one fall about a year after I started ranching, I was going over the Big Belt Mountains on my way home when just on top of the range at the head of Avalanche Gulch, I came onto a camp of a man and woman. The man was the notorious character known as Black Jack Foster. I had known him several years before as a cowpuncher but had not seen him lately. He had married a girl from down in the Missouri River badlands country. He had heard that I was ranching up in that country, and they were on their way to spend the winter with me. After talking with them about thirty minutes, I started to leave. The girl was sitting on a small log beside the fire with a shawl wrapped around her. She was only about sixteen years old. She began to cry and asked me not to go but to spend the night with them. Jack called me to one side and told me that his wife was expecting a child any time. When I returned to the fire after putting my horse on a picket rope (this was before sheep had gotten into that country and a horse would stay fat on a picket rope), it was getting dark and had begun to snow. It was not cold—just a soft, quiet snow. Their outfit was a two-horse wagon and their bed was made down in the wagon box. Just a few old blankets and not much of anything else.

It was not very long before the girl began to feel bad, very much frightened, and was taking on at a terrible rate. Jack and I put her in the wagon. I did not know any more about such things than just the instinct that God had given me. She or Jack didn't either. She was sore at her husband and didn't want him around. So I had to take charge. I am not going into details but it was a hard stunt for a bachelor.

After the baby was born I took it to the fire where I had warm water, washed and dressed it, and put it beside its mother. It was a boy. I left for the ranch in the morning and fixed up an old cabin for them, and in a few days they arrived. The child was all right and healthy. When I saw him last he was six or seven years old.

CHAPTER SEVENTEEN

ADVENTURES WITH BEARS

WHILE I WAS STILL HEADQUARTERING in Jackson Hole, I was in Tobacco Plains one summer when several officers of the law came up there to make some arrests. The Plains are on the line between Montana and Canada, on the Kootenai River. I don't know just what kind of lawbreakers they were after but there was a choice lot of criminals in that district. They could have taken their pick among train robbers, horse thieves, bank robbers, and smugglers of opium or Chinamen. But the officers met with hard luck right at the start. Their horses were all stolen on the first night; they were set afoot and were not able to secure any more horses, and walked over one hundred miles to Kalispell. The logs were so big on this trail that often notches were cut into them for the horses to jump through. I never thought that territory was quite ready to accept civilization.

The incident of the officers made quite a lot of noise. The law-abiding gentry didn't like it. We were notified by the grapevine telegraph that a large posse was coming to clean up the Plains. Now the outlaws were not afraid of the posse, for some of the best shots of the West were there, and it was an easy country to ambush anyone in and get away. It was all anyone could desire in that respect. I will say "we" because I was there and was asked to take part in what might be called a mass meeting. After we got through "making medicine," the bandits decided not to have any trouble or kill anyone, but to get out of there, which they did. Some went east toward St. Marks and the headwaters of Belly River; others went over the range into what is now Glacier National Park. A few with myself followed the Kootenai River. There were only Indians and a few settlers (squaw men) left there.

My party went down the Kootenai River to the mouth of Libby Creek, then about ten miles up the creek where we camped. It was there that the mountain lions killed the prospectors. The next day after making camp I shot a bear running away from me in the river bottom. I struck him in the hip and the bullet lodged in his stomach. We were obliged to kill meat almost every day, as the blowflies were something awful. I have taken lighted sticks from the fire at night and held them up into the brisket of a deer hanging up by his neck. In this way I have killed a full quart of flies, and eggs in bunches as large as baseballs.

We were generally short of cooking grease as the deer were poor. The main reason for shooting the bear was for his oil. The weeds were big and fresh grown which made trailing easy. I followed him for perhaps half a mile where he went into the river, and I could see his wet trail on a gravel bar where he had come out on the other side. The river looked pretty bad and the water, ice cold, came out of snowbanks a few miles farther up, but I made up my mind to try it.

I was pretty heavily loaded. We were always expecting trouble in that country so I had besides my rifle a full belt of cartridges and a .45 six-shooter. I took off my shoes, leggings, and pants, hung my shoes, leggings, and six-shooter around my neck, rolled up my pants and put them under my arm. The gun was used for a prop to hold against the current. I started crossing on a riffle with a very deep hole just below and soon saw that I had made a mistake in taking off my shoes. The pebbles would wash out from under my feet and I could scarcely walk. The distance across was about one hundred yards.

About the middle, I realized I couldn't make it. The water was about up to my shoulders; the stones were all going out from under my feet. I tried to take a step backward but was swirled off my feet into the deep hole. I still had my pants under my left arm and the gun in my right hand.

Trying to swim, with one hand with the gun in it and a heavy six-shooter around my neck, was too much for me. I couldn't get my mouth out of the water long enough to get enough breath so I had to let my pants go. That helped some on the breathing, but I was cold and numb. I was making for the end of a long pole, which stuck out from the bank about twenty feet, the end bobbing up and down in the water. I finally got there and got hold of the pole with my left hand. How I did blow. I held on for about a minute and picked out a place where I thought I could land on a little gravel bar, just above a big log jam, which reached nearly across the river. In letting go of this pole I had to go under the water to get by and lost my shoes and hat.

I made the gravel bar, slowly crawled out and laid there, unable to stand up. It was about three miles to camp, and I was on the same side I went in on. I took my leggings which were canvas, rubbed myself until I was fairly warm, then tied them around my feet and headed for camp.

It may seem as though that experience would have been enough, but after a night's rest I still wanted that bear and in the morning left to go after him again. I crossed the river on a log from a short way below where I had been the night before. That was a country of tall trees—nearly all of them over one hundred feet high.

I took up his trail at the gravel bar where he had crossed the river the day before, and about one-quarter of a mile farther on, found him dead. He had been dead for twelve or fifteen hours and was badly flyblown. Nevertheless, I cut him open and took all the fat I could get and some of the fattest meat to fry out for oil. We never brought much meat to camp unless it was killed close by, for the only way to keep it over a day was to put it under running water or take time to jerk it.

I was winding up haying on the ranch in the early part of September one year when I received a letter from an old friend who lived in Helena named Al Odham. Odham was a good hunter. A few years prior to this time Odham with a party of friends who were touring the Yellowstone Park were attacked by a band of Nez Percé Indians, headed by Chief Joseph. Odham was shot through both cheeks and left to die. One woman was taken prisoner. Odham, after several days of hardship, was picked up by a rescue party. The young woman was turned loose after being with the Indians some time.

Odham at this time had an Englishman in tow who wanted to kill a bear, and he asked me if I could go with them. I wrote him that I would be through haying soon and for him and his friend to come over. They came and we rigged up a couple of pack horses, went over across Deep Creek and up a creek called Tenderfoot. We got where I wanted to camp about an hour before night, and while they were making camp, I prospected a little for game.

About a mile above camp was a big sort of bald ridge that had been burned off a few years before and was covered thick with little dead jack pines as large as a man's wrist. The ground was covered with low huckleberry bushes with quite a good crop of berries. I ran into a lot of fresh bear signs within a short time and eased back out of there without disturbing anything. The next morning we were on our way at daybreak. Odham and the Englishman went up the ridge, while I went just a little farther across a small ravine into thick, green timber and kept pace with them. I had not gone far when I saw an immense old cinnamon bear, feeding on berries. The other men could not see him yet. I eased along, keeping both men and the bear in sight. When they got to a point where they could see him, they both dropped flat on the ground and I could see Odham patting the Englishman on the back and whispering instructions in his ear.

The Englishman was badly excited, and it looked as though Odham was having some trouble in keeping him there. The bear was about a hundred yards away and excitedly tramping around on his hind feet. Finally they both raised on their knees, Odham still whispering in his ear, and then the Englishman shot. The old bear raised up about eight feet tall and began madly to wave both front paws around and to bawl, which sounded about like a mad bull.

The bear immediately started down the mountain, directly toward the two men, tearing down the little dead pines as he went, making a terrible noise. I don't think the bear had yet seen any of us, but was just going somewhere.

140

I began running toward them and shooting as I ran. Odham also began to shoot. We had both shot the bear through, and he began to slow up and stagger, partly falling and sliding down the mountain. He stretched out dying, about twenty feet from the other two men.

I got there a few seconds after the bear quit breathing, and the Englishman had thrown down his gun and was sitting flat on the ground with a little quaking aspen tree, about the size of your wrist, between his legs and with both arms around it. He was repeating rapidly: "Get up here, Mr. Odham, you'll be perfectly safe." We found the Englishman had shot the bear through the front paw, but we made him believe that it was his shot that had killed him. He was very happy and well satisfied, though he insisted that he had had a narrow escape.

I left the Freeman Creek ranch one morning about sunup to go over on the head of Rock Creek to look over some cattle. It was early fall, about the middle of the nineties. I took Jeff with me, as there were some large patches of heavy timber where I was going and I could put Jeff in the timber to run the cattle out, which gave me a better chance to look them over.

Jeff was a very intelligent, large shepherd dog, the kind that had dewclaws on his front legs. My neighbors called him my hired man. I used him in the corrals when working cattle by myself. I could put him in an open gate to watch it and when I would bring up the animal I wanted out, I would motion him out of the way. After the one I wanted passed through, Jeff would jump back into the open gateway and prevent any others from getting out.

While riding this time of year, I usually carried an extra lash rope from a pack saddle, which had a cinch and open hook on one end, as I nearly always killed a deer or antelope during the day. The lash rope was used to make them fast to the saddle.

As I came out of the timber on top of the divide between Freeman Creek and Rock Creek there was a patch of snow which was left from a snowstorm of about ten days prior to this. Jeff was ahead of me and had discovered a bear track going across this patch of snow. I got down and examined the track. It was not a very large bear, and the track was fresh and Jeff was wanting to go.

Now Jeff was good at slow-trailing deer and would catch and hold a wounded one, but as far as I knew he had never met a bear. He trailed the bear slowly down the top of the ridge about as fast as my horse would walk. On the left and just over the top of the mountain was some timber; on the right side it was rather open, steep, and rocky and covered with bunch grass. I was riding a small, cropped-eared, red-colored horse which I had bought that summer from an Indian. He was very gentle and one of those good little diggers who are very handy to have around the ranch in winter. I had packed an antelope or two on him but didn't know what he knew about a bear.

I had followed the trail down the ridge a half or two-thirds of a mile and had jumped the bear without seeing him. Jeff broke away and took down the mountain side as fast as he could run. On the opposite side of the gulch was heavy timber. It was only two or three hundred yards to the timber. I left my horse and followed as fast as I could. I had just dropped my bridle reins when, about two-thirds down to the bottom, I could hear Jeff and the bear fighting in the timber, but by the time I got there they were gone.

The ground, which was soft, black dirt and pine needles, was badly torn up and showed that they had had quite a fight. I could hear Jeff squealing a little while he was running, but by the time I got out of the timber I saw Jeff go over the top of the ridge from which I had just come.

Well, I followed as fast as I could, but when I reached the top all was quiet. I turned toward the timber on the mountain side and in crossing a patch of snow, saw where they had gone on a dead run. A short distance from there I could hear Jeff barking up, just like a dog that had a coon treed. I soon got to where I could see him under the tree. I eased along slowly, looking through the tops of the trees, which were large fir trees. I soon saw the bear; he was standing with his hind feet on one limb and front paws over another, very much like a man standing up.

When within about forty yards of the tree I shot him in the breast. He fell end over end, breaking off several big limbs as he fell, and barely missed falling on Jeff, who immediately jumped onto him, biting and pulling and having a good time.

I let Jeff pull him around until he was satisfied. I think the bear was dead when he hit the ground. He weighed around 250 pounds, was very fat and in prime condition. I wanted the oil from the bear to mix with elk and deer tallow. When mixed about half and half it makes a very good substitute for lard or cooking grease.

I took out his entrails and then went back for my horse. I had some little trouble in catching him as my hands smelled of the bear. All range horses raised in the mountains seem to be very much afraid of a bear. I realized I was going to have some trouble getting the meat on Croppy, who began to whistle and cut up when within about one hundred yards of the bear.

Near by was a down tree which had some big limbs near the top. I built a hackamore on Croppy with my saddle rope (a hackamore is very much like a halter), then put my black

143

sweater over his head to blindfold him; finally I got him backed up into the treetop with his rump against the tree in a crotch. I then tied his head tight on both sides. He could not move around very much. I got the bear up on the log and worked it up over the horse's rump and nearly had it into the saddle when he began to take notice and wound up with the bear under his feet. He did a lot of stamping, squealing, and generally raised the dickens. Jeff was trying to help out, which did not help any.

I finally got the bear out from under him, got the horse all straightened out and tried it again; this time I got the bear into saddle and made it stick. I couldn't throw a diamond hitch over him because it takes two men to put on a diamond hitch. I tied him with what we called a "squaw hitch" or "one-man diamond." It was very difficult to tie him on account of the tree and limbs.

I led him out of the treetop before I pulled the blind off. Well, he went to bucking and kicking. I had a long rope on the hackamore and held him in a circle. The bear was so heavy that Croppy would nearly fall down. I let him buck until he was tired out and ready to quit. I didn't have an extra rope to tie the bear's legs, and they whipped Croppy all over while he was bucking.

I got home just before sundown, having fooled around all day with the bear. There were some friends from Helena stopping with me at the time, and a young lady named Miss Nealy Hoagg took our picture—Croppy, the bear, and myself. I still have the picture.

Many years later I spent a winter in Alaska. One day coming down a big creek I saw a bear on the opposite side of the creek from me. His hind feet were on the bank, and his front ones were on a small log that lay from the bank into the creek. I had never seen a bear like this one before;

his body was smooth and round and about the size of a ten-gallon keg. His neck was bigger than his head. His hair was very short and smooth. I stopped and we looked at each other for probably a full minute; then he slowly turned his hind feet onto the ground, walked a few steps, and then loped into the woods. He had been catching fish.

I guess here is as good place as any to tell about the time I was run over by a bear. It was another September during the nineties. It had been snowing all day long and had cleared up in the night, making about eighteen inches of all new snow. The morning after the storm was clear and bright. The wind had not yet started to blow, and snow lay on all the tree limbs and bushes from a few inches to a foot in depth. I left the ranch on Freeman Creek to go over to the South Fork to hunt deer. The sun had just come up as I reached the top of the range where I could look across the South Fork Basin. The far side of the basin was about one mile from me; a little brush branch which was very steep on the far side of the basin divided the bunch grass from the timber. The ground was just as white as snow could make it. Across the basin at the far side I could see a track of something coming down the mountain close to the timber.

This may seem a little farfetched to a person who does not know the mountains; but to show you how it works, I could stand in front of my cabin on Freeman Creek at sunrise after a fair-sized snowstorm and look to the head of the creek, which was also a basin rimmed around by big mountains, and see deer tracks. This was a mile and a quarter from me by the section line.

The deer trailing into this county would pass along just above a big cut bank near the top of the range, which had been caused by a landslide. It was at that point that I could see the tracks.

I kept riding toward these tracks until I was in the bottom of the gulch, then left my horse and walked up the branch to where the tracks crossed into the timber. They were bear tracks. Business began to pick up and I felt sure that he could not get away from me in all that snow.

I got into his trail and followed along the same branch he had come down; only we were on the other side and in the timber. The snow lay several inches deep on all the limbs and you could not see very far. I traveled very slowly and carefully as I felt that the bear had not seen me; and I expected to kill him when he jumped. But presently, while peeking through a little opening and over some of the bushes in the branch, about a hundred yards above me I saw what looked like the end of a haystack, very reddish in color. In a few minutes, without moving, I saw that it was the bear working on his den under a log jam, scratching out rotten wood and dirt, throwing it down the bank on top of the fresh snow, making it look like a dump of dirt at the mouth of a mine tunnel.

I eased very carefully and very slowly, until I was within fifteen or twenty yards of the mouth of the hole, where I settled down in the snow to wait for him to show up. It looked like a cinch. I didn't think he had a chance. I had sat there probably twenty or thirty minutes, when I figured he knew I was there and he was not coming out. The hole looked perfectly black and I could not see in it at all.

I began to move around, staying on the bunch-grass side out of the timber. I finally got on the top of the den, tramped all around among the big logs which were jammed there, probably by a small cloudburst. The snow was up to my belt so that didn't get me anywhere. I decided to get down in the branch directly in front of the hole and shoot into it. Well, I had gotten down in front at the bottom of the dump. I was in quite a good deal of bushes and wanted to take just one more step, to put me right where I wanted to be. I put my left elbow against a bush which was about as big as my wrist, and gently started to push it out of my way. ZOWIE! It let down a big bunch of snow, which fell square on my head and all over me. The bear must have been looking out at me and the fall of snow moved him.

Well, I just had a glimpse of a broad back of a big bear, whose hair was full of red dirt, coming down that dump straight for me. I think he struck me sideways with his body, trying to get out of my way. I went over, landing flat on my back. He seemed to have tramped all over me. I think he had been fooled by the dirt of the snow as it looked like solid ground but it let him down two or three feet more than he expected and he could not help running or falling over me. What I saw was his back. He seemed to be on the back of his neck falling over endways.

I got out of the snow and got straightened out, but no bear was in sight. I never fired a shot. Of course I still wanted him; he was a silvertip and good size. I got his trail and followed him over that mountain side until nearly night, when he crossed the top and headed for Rock Creek. I decided to call it a day. I was wet and cold from perspiration and melting snow. The sun had gone down and I was about two miles from my horse.

Several of us, when riding circle one morning on the Rock Creek roundup, got after a big brown bear. When we first sighted the bear he was moving along a low bald ridge which had a limestone ledge cropping along it. The bear got behind the ledge where we could not see him. By the time we got to the top of the ridge he had run into a thick patch of small fir timber on the north side of the hill. It was only about one or two hundred yards through the timber downhill to a small limestone gulch. On the opposite side of the gulch was a bald hill covered with bunch grass.

I went around the upper end of the timber while two of the boys went around the lower end and one went through, leading his horse. I went down the little limestone gulch. I had gotten about opposite the center of the timber, where the side of the gulch was very steep. At this point it had for ten or twelve feet about a forty-degree slope and very smooth rock. I set my horse down on his tail and slid him down this place. At the bottom was a sharp curve. On one side was perpendicular rock and on the other side, a ten-foot bank.

It was at this point that I met the bear. He came sliding down from the top of the bank almost under my horse's feet. He was looking backward for the men in the timber. My horse was still sitting on his tail and could not get onto all of his feet. The bear was striking frantically with his front paws and trying to keep from sliding under my horse. My horse was trying to get up that perpendicular wall. I had a six-shooter in my hand ready to shoot but could not get time for action.

It was all over in a few seconds, and I was going down the gulch on a scared horse without bridle. The bear had pawed it off. A little farther down the draw I was roped by one of the other boys and stopped. The bear got away. There was not a shot fired at him. My horse was scratched a little in the face and on the neck. I don't know which was frightened the most, the bear or my horse. The horse, however, showed a nervousness from it for a week or ten days.

Here is my saddest bear story; it makes me feel badly yet whenever I think of it: After a big early snow I had gone over to the south fork of Freeman Creek to kill some deer.

148

I was wallowing through the snow which was above my knees, going up a side ridge which was covered with down logs and few small live fir trees all having about a foot of snow on them. Looking to my right across a narrow steep little draw and about two hundred yards away, I saw the back of a big silvertip bear. I dropped in the snow. In a few seconds he raised his head, shook off the snow, looked around a few seconds and again went to rooting in it. He was eating kinnikinnick berries. As soon as he lowered his head I began to crawl to a place where he could not see me. He was a little below me and just at the lower edge of a bad spruce and fir thicket which reached to the top of the mountain. Just below him was a clump of dog spruce trees (that is the kind that has long limber boughs and very heavy foliage). The limbs were weighted down with snow and presented a solid wall which you could not see through or under.

I crawled most of the way and got across the little gulch into the edge of the sapling thicket and worked down, getting as close to him as I could without scaring him. I wanted this grizzly and no mistake about it. When within about one hundred feet of him and his head was down in the snow, I got onto my knees and when he raised his head, shot him in the butt of the ear. I raised up and saw the bottoms of all four feet just as though a horse was rolling over, going slow. I said to myself outloud, "Oh, how easy," and started to walk toward him.

I had only taken a few steps when a bear went tearing out from the lower side of the dog spruce, going in a quarter-circle around me, making for the fir thicket. I had only a few seconds' time to see him but shot him through the body and took after him as fast as I could run, trying to turn him from the thicket or get another shot, but did not do so. Blood was running out of both sides of him. The thicket had so

149

many down poles and the growth was so stiff it was almost impossible to get through. You could hardly get through to the ground anywhere but had to crawl from pole to pole. I could not see any of the prints of the bear's feet, just places where he had knocked the snow from overhead and off of the down timber. The small, wiry spruce trees were as thick on the ground as wheat in a field.

The chase started shortly after sunrise. I followed that bear until about the middle of the afternoon; he never went out of the thicket. By this time the snow had gotten softer and I began to see a few of his footprints. I made up my mind that this wasn't the bear I had first shot at all; his feet were too small.

I left this trail and went clear back down to the spot where I had stood when I first shot, then walked over to where the bear had rolled over but could not see him. I then went around the other side of the dog spruce. The snow there was all rooted up by the bear. I hurried back up the mountain again to pick up the trail where I had left off.

The sun by this time was over the mountain and it had begun to freeze. I was wringing wet from perspiration and snow. The bear could be heard ahead of me a good part of the time but could not be seen. It began to get dark in the thicket and I had to give him up.

The next day I left with a four-horse team for Helena, to get a load of grub for the winter. I was gone two weeks, and during that time the thought of that bear never left me. The snow by then was pretty well out of the valleys.

The morning after my return to the ranch, I went over on the South Fork and straight to where the bear had been. The ground was all bare—no snow at all; the bows of the spruce were lifted up and I could see under them. The weeds and grass were all flattened down; the ground was saturated

150

with bear grease and a mat of hair. There lay his backbone just under the bows. It was about the length of a cow or horse backbone, with the skull on the neck. The rib bones were all chewed down nearly to the backbone. The hair from his mane measured six to eight inches long and was as soft as silk. When shot, he had rolled under those dog spruce trees and been completely covered with snow.

I was almost sick about it. I twisted his skull off and had started back down when over on the left I saw some magpies making a fuss and a coyote standing on the hillside. I shot him. Went over that way and there lay the other bear all eaten up, about three hundred yards from where I had quit his trail. The ground was soaked with grease and hair about the same as the other. He was about two years old. I took the two skulls home with me. I still feel bad about those bears.

CHAPTER EIGHTEEN

MONTANA GAME AND PREDATORS

IN SEPTEMBER, the Montana blacktail deer are in their best condition for meat. Their necks have not yet started to swell, and the fat on their rumps squares one inch. This was the time of year that I usually killed my winter meat. After the first of November, a buck deer's neck would be swelled and the meat tough and strong. However, if the meat with the hide on was thrown in a snowbank and left for a month or more, it would become very tender and sweet.

A blacktail deer when walking in snow drags his feet, just shoves them along, going very slowly and making tracks that show as plain as a man's. But when you jump him on a mountain side in rough country or down timber, he very much resembles a bouncing rubber ball, keeping all four feet together, making a track not much larger than a pack rabbit and hitting the ground twelve to fifteen feet apart. I did not hunt deer for sport, only for needed meat.

Near my home there was a big, dry, timbered mountain where I often went to kill blacktail deer. Very often, when only a short way up the mountain, I would be met by some magpies. The magpie is a very intelligent bird and a meat eater. He lives in Montana all year round. The birds would fly around me, making a lot of fuss, then lead out, flying short distances, and wait for me. They would usually lead me to a band of deer lying down. The magpies would get theirs after the killing was over.

There is a country lying north of Kalispell and about 110 miles from Tobacco Plains by the old trail. It was a very heavily wooded country and the haunt of literally thousands of whitetail deer. I don't think there was ever a place in North America that had so many deer in it for the same amount of country. Near the Plains were some mule-tail deer, also hundreds of mountain lions and a good many bear; it was a hunter's paradise.

On Libby Creek, about a day's ride over the Kootenai River trail from the Plains, is the only place I have known mountain lions to attack a man. There were three men prospecting about ten miles up the creek from the river. A lion jumped on one of them in daylight. He was driven off before the man was killed, but he was badly hurt. The two men then started toward camp with the wounded one but had to stop in the woods. The wounded man and one other remained in the timber overnight. When several men arrived the next day to bring the wounded one in, they found that the lions had killed both men during the night, even though they had scattered pieces of burning wood in every direction. Fire will generally keep wild animals at bay.

There is a big chicken hawk in the Northwest called the "hen hawk." When the young are about the size of squabs they grow a fleece of wool, which is from a half-inch to an inch in length and white in color—not a feather on them.

153

At this stage they weigh from *six to eight pounds*. Full-grown birds weigh less than *three pounds*. If you are short of meat the young birds are very good to eat.

A mountain rat is peculiar. He seems to want to meet you halfway. He will take anything out of the cabin that he can move: knives, forks, spoons, small dishes, and cartridges. I have known them to pack off eggs and have tracked them to their cache and recovered them. When he takes anything out he usually brings something back in return—sticks, bones, stones and any old dry thing that he can find—that's why he is sometimes called the "trade rat."

If you set a small, bright, steel trap for him and he doesn't happen to get into it, he will carry it off. He seems to have a sense of humor. At nights while you are sleeping he will get up on a plate log and jump down on you, usually lighting in your face. He is responsible for the prospector's habit of sleeping with his hat over his face. The rat is about the size of a month-old kitten, with big ears, very wise-looking face, flat body, and flat tail. The hair on the tail lays flat and has the appearance of being parted in the middle. He makes his home in big limestone ledges. During the summer he fills all the caves and crevices with small cut brush. I have seen what would make a small hayrack load of brush in a single cave. He can climb up a vertical, smooth, rock surface. He holds his tail against the surface, and it seems to help him.

He delights in getting hold of your saddle rope or harness, which he will cut to pieces, similar to a porcupine. If you have been absent from your cabin, say for a month or more, you will find your fireplace and bunk full of sticks, bones, any anything that the rat could find to bring in. I have had one sit on the ridge log and watch me clean house. They are found from Alaska to the Mexican border. Indians like to eat pack rats and will tell you: "He all same chicken."

154

Part of the time during the nineties, Montana paid twenty-five dollars bounty per head on wolves—the state paying part and the North Montana Roundup Association paying some.

I had not been ranching long enough to have very many steers of the beef age yet, and cash monty was quite an item; so I did some wolfing—not only for the money, but I enjoyed the sport of destroying the brutes. A friend of mine named John Hopkins, who lived on Deep Creek, which is the west end of Smith River in Meagher County, had a pack of about fourteen large, stiff, wiry-haired stag hounds, which were of the Russian variety and very vicious.

It was dangerous for a man to whip one of these dogs as he was very apt to attack you. We handled them with a long cracking bull whip, usually while on a horse. I was associated with these dogs every day for two months more or less, but I don't think that one of them ever showed any friendship or in any way recognized me. One or two of them at rare intervals wagged his tale at Hopkins. It is my opinion that a cross of these stags with a wolf would produce a more vicious animal than the wolf itself.

Hopkins came and spent a good part of one winter with me, and we had many a lively chase. If the dogs would catch a wolf in the open, they would kill him and tear him to pieces in short order. You could hardly see the animal for dog heads when they would all get hold of him and start pulling him to pieces, and they would just about eat him up if you didn't get there within a few minutes. Sometimes the hide would be so badly torn up you could hardly get enough of it together to get the bounty on it—namely, the scalp with ears attached. However, if the wolf was up against a cut bank, under logs or partly in some hole where they couldn't get behind him, it was hard for them to kill him

155

without our help. These stags weighed from seventy-five to about one hundred pounds each.

Quite often a wolf would get hold of a dog and give him a bad cut, though we never had a dog killed. Just to show you the viciousness of these brutes, I mean the dogs, if they got loose during the night, which they sometimes did, they would generally wind up in the big pasture field killing one or more calves about the same as a pack of wolves would have done. I have known them to kill a weaned calf in the pasture field and gorge themselves with meat and curl up in the snow to sleep, very much the same as wolves would do. They were fast enough to catch a jack rabbit but were not allowed very often to run one.

One of the pack was the mother of part of them. We called her "Grandma." One morning we left her shut up in the barn on account of sore feet. She climbed up into the hay-loft and got out and followed us. She didn't come up to us but stayed behind a half-mile or less.

We had one hound dog in the pack who would trail. He had just struck a trail of something and we turned the pack loose. They would follow the hound until something was jumped, as they only run by sight. We had not seen the old mother dog and didn't know who was following us until the pack sighted her about a half-mile away on a ridge behind us and broke for her. We could not stop them. They went straight for her. She laid down with her head between her paws and didn't move. We had to go out of our way around a rock cliff, which made us slow. When we got there they had killed their mother.

The most wolves I have ever seen in one pack, I saw that winter. We counted twenty-two wolves go over a ridge. It was nearly dark and we were afraid to turn the dogs loose, but left them with an Indian who was hunting with us. We got among them with our horses and guns and killed five before they got into a rough and rocky timbered country around Black Canyon and scattered. Our dogs could not run in heavy timber. A pack of from three to six wolves made a very interesting chase. Usually there were only three of us, and sometimes there would be a lone dog after one wolf. The dog would bay him, but we would have to shoot the wolf as the outcome of a fight was always doubtful. A good dog could kill a poor wolf, but I don't remember of one dog ever killing a prime wolf.

We jumped and caught a two-year-old bear one day. The dogs tore him to pieces. They could catch and eat a badger in less time than it takes to tell it.

A wolf, like most range animals, can smell a blizzard or real cold spell coming from twelve to twenty-four hours before it strikes, and they will be very active and sassy during that time. If you are riding on the range a day before a bad storm, you will see them in evidence more or less all day long. I mean, you will see a wolf or coyote several times during the day.

I came onto a pack of five wolves one evening just before a storm. They had just killed a cow and a hundred, more or less, of range cattle were milling around the dead one, pawing the ground and bellowing. The wolves were sitting on the outside of the circle, not able to get to the dead cow. They were quite sassy and allowed me to get up quite close before they started off. I killed three of them.

As far as I could make out from my observation, I believe nearly all whelps are born in a hole in the ground, usually an enlarged badger hole. Then when about the house-cat size, the mother takes them to a den in the rocks. I have known of several rock dens where whelps have been raised year after year. There was always a variety of bones

157

scattered around. I have seen shoulder blades from large cow brutes, back bones from sheep, leg bones—both below and above the knee—skulls of large-sized cattle and calves' heads. Also, bones from small animals, such as jack rabbits, lambs, badgers, and others. They were usually chewed up except the skulls.

The mother will drag or carry meat to her whelps, such as a sheep, calf, or part of a cow, until the little ones are large enough to follow. But if the bait is too big or too far away, she will fill herself with meat, then disgorge for the puppies to eat. A mother wolf has been known to drag to her den pieces of meat and bone that weighed about twenty pounds.

One very cold morning near a place called the "Point of Rocks" on Freeman Creek, at a bait where I had caught more than one coyote, I found a large, very healthy wolf in my trap. There was a fence arm laying near which I had used to kill coyotes with. You usually caught several coyotes at the same bait. The arm is used as a brace for a leaning fence and is about the size of a baseball bat and four or five feet long. I struck the wolf between the ears as hard as I could, in order to break his skull, before a blood clot could form. After a blood clot forms it makes a cushion, and you cannot break a wolf's skull with a stick very easily by striking on this cushion.

Well, I thought this wolf was dead and it was cold and I was on my way home, which was about a mile. I decided to skin him at the ranch and so tied him on behind my saddle with just the saddle strings. He weighed around eighty or ninety pounds. His teeth were in first-class condition. He was a beauty with a Queen Anne's ruff around his neck, the hair being black and white and about six inches long.

When within about one-half mile of the ranch, my horse

began to cut up and act like he wanted to pitch. I looked behind me; the wolf was very much alive and was clawing my horse with his hind feet on one side, trying to stand up on the other side and had the cantle of my saddle in his mouth, biting and twisting and raising sand. My horse by now was cutting up considerably. I pulled a six-shooter and shot him in the ear, without getting off of the horse or untying the wolf. We left a trail of blood on the snow all the way home.

Sometimes you will find a very old wolf running by himself. I have killed that kind and found him to be poor in flesh and have very bad teeth. It looks as though in old age they are driven from the pack. I have tracked him to where he would meet other wolves and they would have a fight. I think they sometimes kill the very old ones, although I have never found one that the others had killed.

The spring following the winter Hopkins and I had been wolfing, the bounty was still high, and the Indian and I were digging out a wolf den which was in the ground. The mother wolf stuck around all the time we were working, sometimes coming as close as fifty yards, and then sitting down and watching us. I felt sorry for her and picked up a gun to kill her, when the Indian said: "No shoot; he catch 'um more papoose."

To please the Indian, I did not kill her. We got twelve small whelps from the den. The bounty was just the same for whelps as it was for grown wolves. I always thought my dog Jeff was the father of those whelps, although at that age they looked like full-blood wolves. My ranch on the head of Freeman Creek was a high, wild country at that time, and on several occasions Jeff was enticed away by the call of the wild.

Wolves usually kill cattle in this way: They would get

159

the cattle to running down a steep hillside and one would fall down; they would bite him in the flank just ahead of his hip and could pull some of the entrails out with one bite, cutting clear into the hollow. After a cow had been bit in the entrails, she'd act like she'd been gun shot. They would not show the same vitality that a wild animal does and seldom ever got up again, after falling down. Often, too, a wolf would catch an animal by the nose while running, the wolf swinging clear of the ground, and throw him down, or run him into a snowbank and kill him.

Wolves were very bad about killing colts, but if a bunch of range horses could get a wolf surrounded on good ground, they nearly always killed him by striking and kicking him. A band of mares with a lot of young mules two or three years old among them were the worst after a wolf or coyote. The mules would sometimes give chase very much resembling a pack of dogs, and if the wolf could not get into shelter within a short distance, they would usually kill him. I have known horses actually to stomp on a wolf after having him down. A stallion would not let a wolf come near his band of mares.

Wolves in winter, after filling up on something they have killed, will generally go into a heavy patch of timber high up where the snow is deep and round out a hole just big enough to get into; there they will lay all day long. Wolves traveling in deep snow will walk one behind the other, Indian style, all stepping in the same track, which will not look much larger than if made by one wolf. Wolves seem to have a little system in their marauding raids and would come back over the same territory at fairly regular intervals.

While riding on the beef roundup one fall north of Shelby Junction, myself and one other cowpuncher roped a wolf. We led him into Shelby between us and traded him to the barkeeper for a round of drinks.

CHAPTER NINETEEN

I NEVER GOT ALONG WELL WITH SHEEP

SPEAKING OF SHEEP, sheep and I never got along well together. The only fun I ever had with sheep was riding the old rams around the barnyard when I was a boy.

Cowpunchers and sheepherders have very little in common. About the only time they ever mix is when a bunch of cowboys try to eat all the grub in a sheep camp. The sheepherders were good for other things besides herding. They could usually be depended upon to file a homestead or desert claim on a water hole and fence it, *this* way: with two wires high enough so sheep could go under but so it would turn wild cattle. That was when cowpunchers added wire cutters to their outfit.

Sheepherders sometimes kick about their grub. I heard old Elick McDonald, who was a camp tender for a big outfit that ranged out our way in summer, tell a herder who was kicking about the grub: "You haven't been here six months until you are kicking about the grub. You get better grub in a Montana sheep camp than you get in Scotland at a picnic."

A sheep is like this: when cutting his throat before butchering him, he never makes any noise. I always thought he knew he had it coming, so didn't holler.

Just an incident: it was early fall, and two prominent lawyers and a former judge of Helena, Montana, and myself were on our way to the headwaters of Sun River to hunt elk. We had a double-box dead ex-wagon, were driving four horses and a lead saddle horse. My part of the job was to drive the team and keep the camp in meat. The other men furnished the other ingredients; among them was a gallon bottle, which had been filled by the expert behind the bar of the Lambs Club, with ready-mixed Manhattan cocktails. Well, this was the second day out and it didn't taste so good as it did the night before, and we didn't mind giving some of it away, as we had plenty of good liquor.

We had just turned the top of a hill where we could look down onto Rock Creek, where we intended to camp for the night. We drove right into a band of sheep which filled the road.

The Judge was quite a josher and wanted to talk to the herder, so we stopped. A conversation something like this took place:

"Good morning, sir," says the Judge. "You have a very nice-looking band of sheep. We have no fresh meat and would like to buy one."

"Nothing doing, old-timer," says the herder. "I'm paid to look after these sheep and as long as I am in charge nothing like that will ever happen."

"That's fine, young man. It does me good to meet a man of your type. Not often met with in these places, so will be going. Just a minute; Bill, hand me that bottle which is just behind that saddle." Then turning to the herder, the Judge continues: "My friend, this is something just a little special which we had put up before leaving Helena. I wish

162

you would try a little of it," passing the bottle out to the herder.

The swig he took from that bottle would have felled an ox. His eyes brightened up, he shook himself and started in with a lot of conversation. I started the team and we moved on down to Rock Creek, the herder following alongside of the wagon.

While we were getting into camp the Judge and the herder were sitting off to one side with the bottle between them. The Judge called me to them shortly, saying: "Crawford, our friend here has decided to let us have a mutton." The herder got up very unsteadily on his feet, and with a good deal of jesture with his arms, said "You are all my friends. I have seven thousand dollars worth of property here in my charge. It's all yours or any part of it that you want, nothing is too good for my friends." I got the mutton. Just at dark I took his dog and rounded up his sheep and bedded them down. He came to sometime after midnight and hunted up his sheep. But he forgot to come and tell us good-by in the morning.

It is my private opinion that sheep have done more real damage to the semidesert lands of the West than any other thing that man could devise. Of course, we must have wool and some people even eat the meat and say they like it. Being a cowman I never got that way. If there is anything that looks like pest or scourge to a cowman, it's when he sees a band of sheep coming over the hill near his home ranch. Grasshoppers, locust, crickets, or anything is preferable. He knows that in a few years he must move out; his range will be a desert. Before the sheep got there, in certain parts of the West you could keep a horse fat on a picket rope. After sheep came a ground squirrel could hardly make a living.

163

After the advent of the high tariff on wool, it only took a few years to turn the trick. At about that time I lobbied around the Montana legislature trying to get some kind of an act through that would regulate the number of sheep on the land, that would not overstock the range and destroy the grass, something like the law of Alberta, Canada. However, the sheepmen were too many for me; I didn't get anywhere.

The sheepmen have three times a year to bring home the bacon; namely, lambs, wool, and mutton. In the old days it took a cowman four or five years to produce a beef. The sheep win.

The sheep outfitters figure something like this: all the range near his home ranch is his winter and spring range for lambing; all the faraway range and high country is his summer range. The old cow kept getting poorer and poorer each year until you couldn't finish a beef outside of a fence. About that time the war started. I mean the sheep war, with every band of sheep sent up into my country. They had escorts of about two men with Krag-Jörgensen rifles. It was quite exciting but that's another story.

The buffalo grass on the Plains and benchlands, and the bunch grass in the foothills works something like this; they only reseed during favorable seasons from three to five years apart and will only live a few years longer if not allowed to reseed. Sheep eat the grass very close and leave very little for reseeding. In the winter they paw through the snow. After they have gone over it a few times there is little left except a few roots.

When the price of wool is up they breed so fast, a sheepman just naturally can't help overstocking the range. He keeps all she-stock until their teeth drop out. He has done his bit toward creating the "Dust Bowl."

In late years he has been obliged to go into the very high

country, I mean sometimes above the timber line. He leases, rents, or pays so much per head for the right to graze on some forest reserve. He gets this right from some of our various agricultural departments. I understand the rent he pays hardly pays the wages of the government man who looks after him. Anyway, this is the damage sheep do: they eat up every vestige of vegetation that grows, all the way up through the timber and beyond to the top.

Now this country he has passed through and over is the home of nearly all of our game animals, birds, and even fish. The few ptarmigan, fool hens, blue grouse, and pheasants that are left haven't got a chance. Their nesting places are disturbed; all of their summer food, which is principally berries for the young birds, such as wild strawberries, huckleberries, kinnikinnick berries, and some patches of chokecherries and a few others, all are gone. The old mother grouse whose winter food is pine needles can get along for a few years, but there is very little increase. Hence their doom.

Deer are constantly disturbed and chased about and will not do well. The vegetation is gone, taking with it most of the protection the snow had, so it melts early, runs off quickly; and there will be a shortage of water in the early summer, when most needed for irrigation. The water going out in a hurry is muddy and extra high, taking with it a great many trout that never get back.

To me the sheep is menace No. 1. The only solution I see to save our wildlife is to compel the men who own sheep to keep them on their own land, which would only be fair competition to the men in the East who have sheep. Or the New Deal might take them over and feed them on that thirty million acres of land they are taking out of production.

Cattle and horses on the range, unless it is very badly

overstocked, will leave enough grass to reseed and would be a very long time in destroying the range. I have taken into my ranch lost bands of sheep and their herders during bad weather and blizzards, and saved them from freezing. I don't now why I did it; it's just my way.

For example, one time on a comparatively warm morning in October, I had gone from the ranch over on South Fork of Freeman Creek to hunt blacktail deer. By the middle of the day I was probably two miles from my horse, when it began to snow and blow and soon turned into a blizzard. As soon as I could get to my horse I left for home. While crossing the range, on a trail I had cut through a spruce thicket on top of the range, I could hear at irregular intervals the bleating of a band of sheep. Sometimes they would appear to be within a hundred yards of me. The sound was mixed up with the storm. It was about two miles straight across the basin from where I was to the rimrocks on the other side where the sheep actually were.

The ranch houses were in the valley below me about one thousand feet lower down and about halfway across the basin. I rode up in front of the door and called one of my men. When he came out I asked him if he had seen any sheep. He answered: "No." We had always had trouble with sheep on the range, and there was a very bitter feeling between cattlemen and sheepmen in general. I said: "I'm going up back of the field as I think there is someone lost up there. There were no sheep allowed on that range.

It was over half a mile to the fence, up a rocky mountainside. The temperature must have been fifteen to twenty below zero, with snow and wind blowing a gale from the northwest. When I got out of the field I saw tracks where the sheep had just drifted by.

I turned with the storm, tracking the sheep as I could

only see a few rods. In a short time I found the herder sitting on a rock with a small flour sack, which he had carried his lunch in, tied around his head. He was crying and stiff with cold. His two dogs were there with him. I got off and helped him to mount my horse. It was all he could do to stay on him. Then I led the horse until the fence could be seen. I told him just to hang on and let the horse follow the fence down to the ranch and that I would get his sheep.

I took his dogs and started on a run; the dogs were keen to go. We soon found the sheep for they had stopped on the edge of a small, steep, sharp coulee, which was already half full of snow. They were milling around afraid to go in. I put the dogs around them and threw them downhill until we struck the fence.

The fence down which I started the sheepherder ran east and turned in a curve down the mountain side going south. The fence that I now had the sheep against came up from the east and turned down at the mountain side to the south, making a wide-mouth V-shaped entrance which terminated in a narrow lane near the corral. I hurried the sheep down the lane without much trouble and got to the corral a few minutes behind the herder, who was by then feeling better. I turned the handling of the sheep over to him while I piloted them around into the cattle sheds.

It was now dark and being early in the fall, there were no cattle around the ranch yet. We got most of the frost out of the herder by snow applications to his feet, hands, and face. By morning he was in pretty fair shape. The next day the weather was so bad we could not get the sheep out but about two hours before night on the second day the storm broke and the herder got the sheep out back of the cabin for a short time.

Next morning was clear and calm and the herder left with

his sheep. We helped him to the top of the divide by breaking trail through big drifts with saddle horses. We learned later of other bands that were lost or badly scattered with many dead in that storm, and that several herders were frozen to death. During my time there on the ranch I took in three different bands of sheep and their herders during blizzards.

There seemed to be quite a large percentage of sheep-herders that would become loco or go bugs, usually on the subject of religion. With two companions, we were eating dinner in my cabin on Freeman Creek ranch one day when we heard someone walk up to the open door. After calling him to come in, and no one came, I went to look. There stood a man, very wild eyed, unshaven, dirty and bad look-ing; he had on his shoulder a fence pole about twelve feet long and about four inches through.

His first words were: "I fear neither man, beast, God, nor the devil."

"I don't either, old-timer. Throw down that pole and come in and eat," I said.

"I am Cain. I am Abel," he said.

"It don't make any difference around here who you are. Come on in," I replied.

About this time I was joined by one of the cowboys. After a few more lines of conversation on religion, we pulled him into the cabin and sat him down at the table. The rough handling seemed to do him good. After he got started on beefsteak, boiled potatoes, and squaw bread, he ate a very hearty meal. Later, we put him on a gentle horse and with an escort of two cowpunchers, took him over the divide to a stage station, ten miles away, where he would be taken care of until taken out.

I was on my way, one Sunday morning, to the post office, which was over the main range and ten or eleven miles away.

On top of the divide, and still on my land, which was not yet fenced, I met a band of sheep coming up the road. I soon met the herder who was in a big hurry to catch up with his sheep. He didn't know me, or I, him. He told me he had written some very important letters which were at his camp. The camp tender had not been to his camp that week and he couldn't mail his letters.

I showed a willingness to go by his camp and get his letters, for which he was very grateful, but he was certain that I could never find his camp. It was about a mile off to one side of my route and I knew where it was as well as he did. He said: "If you will only find my camp and get the letters and mail them, I will do anything in the world for you; but I must hurry, my sheep will soon be on that blankety, blankety Crawford's land, who lives on Freeman Creek. I am not afraid of him but I don't want to have to kill him. Good-by." And he left me, running to catch up with his sheep. I went on to his camp, got his letters, and mailed them.

PART IV

Death Valley Days, 1906–10

CHAPTER TWENTY

I BUY A MINE

IN THE WINTER OF 1906, after ranching for about ten years, I sold the Montana ranch and went to California. Going directly to San Francisco, I missed the great earthquake and fire by two days. Was in Los Angeles when the destruction took place.

That same spring I went into the desert in the vicinity of Death Valley, prospecting. Goldfield was then coming into prominence, Rhyolite and vicinity were having a boom, as were Beatty, Gold Center, Greenwater, Bullfrog, Skidoo, and other places. All of them were going along great and I met a number of the old timers. Some of them were successful. Among these were George Wingfield, Kid Highly, and Bob Montgomery, who were in the millionaire class. During that year I bought a group of claims called the "Cashier" and for four years worked them. They were located in the Panamint Mountains at an elevation of five thousand feet, on Harrisburg Flats. To the eastward about two miles was the rim of Death Valley.

Pete Augleberry and Shorty Harris were the discoverers of the Cashier property. There was a great amount of float rock which ran from seventy-five to one hundred dollars per ton. The ore, when broken up, very much resembled old streaked bars of Castile soap. I always thought from what I had heard of the description of the ore that the Cashier was the famous lost Breyfogle mine. There were the remains of a very old sagebrush bed on top of the outcrop of this high-grade ore.

The Cashier claims were fifty miles from Rhyolite, and to get there one had to cross Death Valley. Our freight and mail came from Johannesburg, which was to the southwest about one hundred miles' distance. For the first two years we packed water on burros from Emigrant Springs, eight miles away. A load was four cans, or twenty gallons to each burro. The Springs made water very slowly and it took all day to get a load.

The Skidoo mine was then doing development work, and was a good camp. They hung one man there by the name of Joe Simpson for the killing of a citizen named Arnold. After the first two years Skidoo got water through a pipeline from Telescope Peak, twenty-two miles away. It crossed my claims and supplied me with water. The altitude of Telescope Peak was eleven thousand feet and the pipeline started at nine thousand. It was some job to put in that pipeline, the wagon haul being about one hundred miles. The last of the way it was dragged by mules and packed on burros. It was nearly all about twelve-inch cast-iron pipe. I understood each length weighed about six hundred pounds. The route was sandy, rocky, mountainous desert, with scarcely any water and no feed. It was a real "he-man" job, done by Bob Montgomery.

Standing on Telescope Peak one could look directly down into Death Valley which was over a hundred feet below sea level, making a hole over eleven thousand feet deep. There is no other such jump-off on earth that I know of. We could see Furnace Creek ranch from the rim, a forty-acre patch of alfalfa which looked about the size of the top of a dining table.

Death Valley Scotty stopped at my camp occasionally. Scotty was always quite a mystery to the prospectors and desert rats, and caused a great amount of conversation among them. Some had followed him and his mules considerable distances at various times but had never gotten very much satisfaction out of it. I never asked him any personal questions. I, together with several others, was with him one day in Los Angeles. We were riding in an open automobile on our way to the Lankersham Hotel on Spring street. Scotty had the car stop and began to tear one- and five-dollar bills in two and throw them into the street. This started a lot of scrambling, jamming, a little fighting; and needless to say we blocked the traffic. He was a grandstand artist, nevertheless, I enjoyed going around with him. He had the respect of all the desert rats that knew him. I have seen him when he would have one or two sacks of very high-grade ore, and I always thought the ore had been gotten from the high-graders of Goldfield or Rhyolite.

The last time I saw Scotty was at Kramer, California, I think in the summer of 1909 or '10. Kramer is west of Barstow, where a branch railroad takes off the main line of the Southern Pacific and goes to Johannesburg. I was waiting for a main-line train.

Scotty was at the section house and had with him four saddle horses and a young man whom he said was the son of Ayres, the sarsaparilla man. He was taking him on a similar trip to the one on which he had taken Rol King, Al Mayers, and others a year or two before, only the Ayres trip was to be a little rougher. He was going up and over the top of Jail Canyon, which is in the Panamint Mountains west of Ballarat. If you take horses up that canyon you must push on them part of the way. It's too steep for a horse to climb without help. Going down the other side into Death Valley is a drop of about eight thousand feet. Going down you must snub your horses to trees or rocks to keep them from falling. I never heard how the trip came out but feel sure it was successful to Scotty's way of thinking. I felt sorry for the boy though, and the weather was, oh, so hot.

During my first winter on the desert there were several of us camped on the Cashier claims. Four feet of snow fell on the flats during one storm; I mean just four feet of snow. We were camped in tents. The snow broke our tents down nearly flat. It was very cold; the only wood we had was small sticks of greasewood and sagebrush very difficult to get, as it was all buried deep under the snow. We suffered a great deal. There was one frame building under construction in the skeleton stage. It was to have been used for a saloon. We started to burn it a piece at a time, and it was finally all burned up that way. The lumber had cost, laid down there, plenty of money.

I think it was on the third morning after the storm was over that we saw my two mules coming into camp. One was standing about two hundred yards away, braying, with just his head and neck sticking out of the snow. He kept pushing and wallowing until he made camp. They had come down from a high ridge where they had been during the storm. By noon we had the mules packed with what stuff we could get along with and made our way toward Death Valley. Within a few miles we were out of the snow. Wood was very scarce in the Valley and we sat up all night, as our blankets were sopping wet.

In the springtime great areas of the desert in that high

altitude are covered with a perfect blanket of wild flowers. They only live a short time. After dying, they dry up and blow away. The desert in and around Death Valley was a very dirty place to live in summer. The hot, dry winds blow the flourlike dust into everything, all through your clothes, hair, eyes, and nose. You couldn't keep clean. You had to breathe on the mouth of your canteen to cool it, to keep from burning your lips, even though you carried it on the shady side of your burro. It was like drinking from the spout of a hot teakettle. The wind felt like it does when you open the door of a hot oven. I have seen two consecutive years without rain or snow.

A handkerchief, washed and held up by the corners, after you had walked fifty feet would be perfectly dry. Very seldom perspiration showed on the surface of your skin. The dryness would bring the heels and toes of a pair of shoes nearly together in a few days if left in a tent without being well protected, and you could never wear them again. A man could live only a few hours without water. It was the land where you climbed for water and dug for wood. The water was high in the mountains and the wood (mesquite bushes), under drifts of sand.

Native provisions were scarce. Our meat was desert rabbits. They were of a reddish brown color, moved about all day long, and were easy to kill. They lived principally on wild squawberries which grew on low thorny bushes. When ripe the berries fell off and dried on the ground. The rabbits ate them in quantities and the meat was nice and sweet. Desert rabbits are somewhat smaller than the northern jack rabbit, but much larger than the cottontail. The only large wild animals I ever saw in the Panamints were bighorn sheep. On two occasions I have killed and jerked the meat of wild burros, i.e., burros that had been turned loose or lost

177

and had gone wild. Their meat was very good, resembling beef. It took a big freight team twenty days to come in from the outside. We couldn't have fresh meat for the camp.

The first two years I was in camp, there were nineteen bodies of men found on the desert. They died mostly from drinking poisoned water. The so-called poison water acted very peculiarly. It was good today and poison tomorrow. It seemed to be more poisonous to anyone who had eaten salt meat. Personally it never did me any harm, and I have drunk and used the water from all of the water holes within a radius of a hundred miles or more in Death Valley. I was on the desert for five years.

Several springs there were called either "Old Man Spring" or "Old Woman Spring," for the reason that old Indian bucks or squaws had been left there in a small wickiup to die. Some of the tribes were given to that custom.

The Indians who inhabited the Death Valley district of the desert had never been confined to any reservation and received no rations from the government. It was always a mystery to me how they could live from what they got off the desert. It certainly was a man's job. Game was scarce; ammunition was high; and there was very little opportunity to make any money, especially before the whites began to develop some of the mineral deposits. An Indian could snare a few rabbits and shoot a few doves and mountain quail from small wickiups (blinds built near the water holes), using bow and arrows. Other meat animals were the chuckawallas (big lizards) and diamondback rattlesnakes.

Pinon nuts and mesquite bread seemed to be the staples. They would gather the pine nuts high in the mountains. The cones, while still quite green, would be put into a fire until they would open up, then the nuts would be shaken out. They are a small, oily, rich nut.

178

Mesquite bread was made from the yellow-meal sub-stance which was gotten out of the seed pods by pounding the pods in a mortar. The seeds were not used; they are so hard you can scarcely break them with a hammer. The bread was baked this way: First the meal was stirred up with water to about the consistency of dough, then buried in the sand of Death Valley for about one day, after which it was considered baked. The bread would keep indefinitely. In order to get off a piece to eat, it had to be broken with an ax or hammer, then soaked in water. It had a very nasty taste and a white man had to be very hungry before he could make it go down. There were some small fish in Furnace Creek. The Indians would catch them, lay them on a rock, cover them with sand, and in a short time they would be cooked and ready to eat.

I am forgetting the ants. There is a big ant on the desert that makes a nest on the ground from two to three feet high. The Indians would catch them by stirring them up and put a tight-woven basket over them. The ants were left in the basket to die. They would curl up and resemble a small dried currant. They had a sort of sour-sweet taste. In the spring there was a plant called "squaw cabbage" which they ate.

The old squaws and bucks were not treated very well by the young ones. I have seen old squaws on cold, stormy nights, when it was snowing, go out of the tipi with only a small piece of an old blanket or a scrap of canvas. They would stick a few pieces of brush together in a way that would partially shed the wind, lie down up against this brush, and spend the night there. No wonder they would enjoy being left alone at some water hole, to die. I have known white men who became squaw men, and would live with these desert Indians and seem to like it.

179

In this part of the desert, during the spring and early summer, there were thousands of large-sized mourning doves. I was scolding one of the Indians for killing doves that time of the year. The Indian then told me they were all "man doves." " 'Squaw doves' all same back home, catch'um papoose, 'man doves' live on desert. He catch'um fat." As far as I could tell, they were all male birds.

There were several species of large lizards on the desert, including the Gila monster, chuckawalla, and others. One day while with an Indian who was sorting ore for me, I pointed to a large lizard which was of a creamy white color, laying on the ore pile; I said to the Indian: "Why you no eat 'em all same chuckawalla?" He replied: "Me no eat 'em, he chuckawalla's brother. He no good."

The Indian showed his savage nature this way: Sometimes the children would bring in several chuckawallas alive. They would tie them up until dark, then build a fire and form a circle around it. They put the chuckawallas in the fire alive, and got lots of enjoyment out of watching them scatter the coals and ashes, getting out. They would recatch them and continue to put them back into the fire until dead, then finish the cooking and eat them.

When I first went to the camp on the Panamints, varmints were very scarce; there were almost no animals there of any other kind than the rabbits described. But toward the last part of my stay, there was a band of Angora goats brought in by a man named Ed Rivers, and kept there for supplying the camp with meat. After the first year of goats, we saw swifts, coyotes, and lynxes.

When the panic of 1907 struck me, all credit stopped and I was broke. The mine was working sixteen men and had considerable high-grade ore blocked out. I had quite a lot of provisions, but no money. There was an old blue-roan saddle horse which had been living on the range for years. I snared him and put my burro saddle on him. When I straddled him he burst the latigo strap and bucked me off, saddle and all. I then tied the saddle on with ropes clear around him, tried him again and stuck. I rode him to Johannesburg (one hundred miles), sold him for twenty dollars, then went to San Leandro, where I talked the Best Manufacturing Company out of fifteen thousand dollars worth of mining machinery, F.O.B.

The blue roan had been a sort of mystery horse. He had been running between the Cashier mine and Death Valley for several years. No one knew when or where he came from. The brand on him was blotched up so it couldn't be made out, and he had never been vented. He probably was a stolen horse when he was brought in there and had become very wild and crafty. He came for water about every third night, slipping up to the water trough which I had at the crossing of the Skidoo pipeline. He would come up very slowly and quietly. The least noise at camp would send him off snorting and blowing on a dead run, and he would not be back for several days.

The stagecoach had stopped running to Ballarat for the time being, and the blue roan looked like the only chance I had to get out of there. One of the miners helped me catch him. We slit a hole in a corner of the cook tent which was the nearest tent to the water trough, then tied enough rope together to set a snare for him, placing it so he could not drink without standing in the loop. He came about three o'clock in the morning very craftily and slowly. While he was drinking we set back on the rope. We had him by both front feet. He fought us like a wild animal, biting and striking and kicking. After considerable "rastling" we got him down and build a hackamore on him and tied him up till morning.

181

The mining machinery I bought in San Leandro included one twenty-five horsepower gasoline engine, one ten horsepower hoisting engine, and a stamp mill. I must have had a unusual amount of faith in my ability at doing things, for before I left camp I put the men to shooting out the foundation for the mill. The framework I intended to get, and did get, from a near-by gulch. I came back from San Francisco on the freight train which brought my machinery, as I had no money to buy a ticket.

At Johannesburg, I persuaded one of the big freight outfits to haul it in for me, and worked as swamper for the twenty-animal team. The distance was 110 miles, and we had to double on all hills, ranges, and the bad sand, also hauling water. The freighter's name was Fred Conley. The price for hauling was fifty dollars per ton. All told, we made three trips taking about twenty-five days each trip, hauling about fifteen tons per trip.

Conley's outfit consisted of two big desert wagons, with wheels seven feet high, tires five inches wide and one inch thick, and were of the ten-ton capacity. The wagons had been built by Alexander McDonald, the man who built the same class of wagon for Borax Smith, of the "Twenty-Mule-Team Borax" advertising. One trailer with two wheels, the body being about fifteen feet long, was the feed cart. You could tie and feed at one time twenty animals at one of these carts. Two or more sacks of barley were emptied in the cart and about one bale of hay broken up. They were fed only once a day, that being at night. I have known mules to work for ten days at a time fed only on barley, no hay, and be none the worse for it.

Many trying things happened while bringing in that machinery. We had been some ten or more days with a twenty-animal team of mixed horses and mules going toward my camp with eighteen tons of freight. We had been traveling since before daylight across the alkali lakes in the Ballarat district, first through heavy sand, then up the Panamint Mountains, doubling back every steep place all day, and were dog tired.

We had reached Wild Rose Spring with just time enough to get the stock watered, fed, and tied to the feed wagon before dark. I started to get supper. It had been an awfully hot day even for that country. The sky was clear where we were, but I heard some rumbling like thunder up toward the head of the canyon; you couldn't see far in that direction on account of the pinon pine trees and mountains. Then we heard a very peculiar noise up the canyon and about one hundred yards away came a perfect wall ten or twelve feet high of sagebrush, sticks, logs, and trash of every kind which had been picked up by the water. It was a cloudburst and was coming fast. We had just time enough to turn our stock loose and run them up the mountain side, which was not very steep at that point. At our campsite, the canyon widened out a little bit and when the wall of water hit us it was only six or seven feet deep.

We could do nothing but stand on the side and watch it roll over our wagons. At first, for perhaps half a minute, we could not see any of the wagons, and the noise was deafening. Then we began to see some of the shining wagon tires as they turned over and showed above the water. The flood soon passed, and within a couple of hours you couldn't get enough water to drink. The wagons didn't go far for the canyon widened into a gulch just a little way below.

We looked over the situation. Where the spring had been there was only a big pile of sand and gravel. We had to sink a shaft five feet deep into the wash before we could get water. We went to the wagons. Some of them still had a few

183

things in them, but nearly everything had been buried and scattered. It was now dark and things looked pretty bad.

This was the last load of my freight to be brought in before starting the quartz mill. My position was like this: I owed twenty thousand dollars in round numbers, and had no money. I had pulled every string I knew of to get this last load together, and I could not start work without a lot of things that were in that load. The men at the mine were about out of grub. I had spent time and money building the road up the canyon and now that was gone.

We had no supper that night. It was then that the thought came into my mind that it was a good time to cash in on the mine. I turned to my partner and said: "Let's go up the hillside and go to sleep." The next morning we went over the ground carefully, dug out some of the grub, which we ate, and I walked to my camp about eight miles distant. I brought back several miners, and by the next morning we were on our way with a good part of our supplies saved.

I finally got the mill up and started to mill ore. In the first thirty days I paid all machinery and freight bills in full, and shortly afterward, all back pay to the miners. The next thirty days I laid up considerable velvet. About this time trouble broke out over the boundary of my claims and ended in my hitting a Frenchman over the head with a six-shooter. The gun was a self-cocker, and when I struck him I unknowingly pulled it off. This shot his hat off and gave him a long scalp wound, but the shot was really accidental. Since more trouble of the same kind would have happened soon, and I had an opportunity to sell out for cash, I did so and went to Los Angeles.

CHAPTER TWENTY-ONE

RECOLLECTING WITH CHARLIE RUSSELL

ONE GREAT PLEASURE I had while in Los Angeles was meeting up with my friend Charlie Russell, the artist. Russ had been down around Mexico somewhere learning all the little details about Mexican riders and their trappings. He had half a notion to illustrate for some magazine. He and I had been "seeing the elephant" on Saturday night, and decided to go to Pasadena on Sunday morning to see an old cowpuncher who lived there whom we both knew.

We took a streetcar over there in the morning and having quite a holdover, with a thirst, started looking for an emporium where we could get service. The best-looking place was the Green Hotel. We walked into the lobby which was full of people, and we hardly knew what to do. From the clerk's counter I handed a post card to Russ. In about a minute he had drawn a picture on it with a few words to match. He handed it to the clerk who looked at it, then at us, wearing a broad smile. He pressed a button; the boy came and showed us the elevator. We reached the room where the bunch was. I handed them the note the clerk had given us. Well, it was Monday morning when we got down out of there, and we didn't see our cowpuncher friend at all. Russell was by far the best storyteller I have ever met.

At this time we met a cartoonist by the name of Mc-Dowell, who worked for the *Los Angeles Record*. He carried us around to an art store where several of Russell's early pictures were on the wall. In the early days Russell did not date his pictures. He walked up to one of them and looked at it carefully; there was no date on it. He turned to me and said: "Kid, do you know where I painted that?" I said, "No." He told me he painted it in the back room of the "Bucket of Blood" saloon in Chinook, Montana, and paid a forty-dollar bar bill with it. The dealer said: "Two thousand dollars is my price for it." The picture was of an Indian, sitting on a knoll on a white horse looking at a wagon train crossing the Big Muddy in the distance.

From the desert in 1907, I made a trip to Montana and was the guest of Charlie Russell at his home in Great Falls. We talked over old times and the early days, when the place was but a small village.

We recalled the afternoon in Great Falls when Russ almost broke up a speaking engagement of Admiral Schley when the latter was on his tour of the country, after the Spanish-American War. The Admiral, Russ, I, and others had a meeting of our own at the same time. Russ was telling stories at the Park Hotel bar, and the Admiral was so much interested that the committee from the speaker's hall had to send for the Admiral the second time before he would leave.

Russ and I and two other boys passed one winter in the nineties in a cabin in Great Falls, Montana, and were not always flush with money. Sometimes we didn't have too much to eat. Occasionally Russ would paint a picture. Then for a time we would be in funds, and would pay up bar bills and other bills.

Russell remembered how I defied the union walking delegate. There was a fence in front of my relative's house, badly in need of paint. I bought a can of paint and set to work. Shortly a stalky man came bustling up and asked me to show my union card. I had never heard of "a card," as we never had anything of that kind on the range. Real men could break into our profession without a card. I asked him what he meant, and he told me I couldn't paint the fence unless I had a union card. I said that I was doing it: "Watch me and you will see me paint it." He said he would stop me and went away.

I walked back to the barn where my saddle was and swung my .45 on, and went back to the painting. Soon he came back with several others and ordered me to stop. I suggested in a not too mild way for them all to stand back out of the way, to get off my walk as I might want to paint it also. They kept off. Russell came along and saw what was going on. He painted a picture of a cowboy wearing sheepherder's spurs, with a six-shooter hanging on him, painting a fence, with a bunch of union-labor men standing back, watching. We got a good laugh out of the incident. I painted the fence.

CHAPTER TWENTY-TWO

DEATH VALLEY WAYS

SINCE THIS STORY is following my trail, I will give you another fifty miles of it on foot. I had spent about two weeks in Los Angeles and traveling pretty fast, for the desert rat is usually endowed with a good thirst. I returned to the desert on the railroad by way of Rhyolite. About the middle of the next morning I hired a team of horses to haul me as far as Daylight Spring, a small mudhole on top of the Funeral Range, twelve miles distant.

Filling my canteen, I started to walk the rest of the way to my mine, nearly forty miles. I went to the left of the road that went by Stovepipe Springs, making the route a little shorter. When I came out of a canyon into the valley and down a heavy boulder wash far enough to get out of the shadow of the mountain, it was dark. I had walked about sixteen miles. I looked back, for some reason, and saw what I thought was a new moon. I had been in the open most of my lifetime and always kept cases on the moon and stars. I couldn't make out how there could be a new moon in the east at that time of night—I had been out the night before in Rhyolite with a bunch of boys and was still a little shaky.

I sat down on a rock and said to myself: "I left Daylight Springs about ten o'clock and have been walking westerly all afternoon; that's bound to be Old Baldy in front of me." I could see the outline of a big mountain on the skyline across the valley. "I am now in the eastern wash of Death Valley, Stovepipe Springs is on my right, Furnace Creek is on my left. I am right, and the moon is wrong." On taking another look at it, I noticed that something was wrong sure enough, and I continued to watch the moon come out from an eclipse.

Daylight found me the next morning on my hands and knees crawling up to Blackwater Springs. This was a little trickle of water that came out of a ledge of rocks and remained on the surface for only twenty or thirty feet. It made only a few gallons of water per hour. The Springs were at about five thousand feet elevation. I had made the trip with an ordinary pair of dress shoes; the soles were completely gone, and my feet were bleeding. My canteen was empty, and I was sure enough dry. After filling up with water, I lay there and went to sleep. I was awakened some hours later by some of my own burros coming for water. I rode on one of them to camp, which was only about three miles away.

The first time I saw Stovepipe Springs, it was this way: I had been told where they were and after looking around quite a bit, I noticed a white jawbone of a burro stuck up in the sand. Printed on it with a lead pencil were the words "Stovepipe Springs." I went to digging and soon found water. This water sometimes killed people who drank it and at other times it was all right. One of the springs, which was rather out of the ordinary, was called "Hole in the Rock." It is located in the foothills back east of Stovepipe, up a dry gulch and on top of a flat limestone cropping. It is just about like a jug, the neck being large enough to put down a water bucket. Usually no water flows over the top. If you bail it dry, watering your stock and filling up your water cans, and spend the night there, it will have twenty or thirty gallons more of water in it in the morning. The jug holds about a barrel and is splendid water.

One morning while at my camp at the Cashier mine, the doctor from Skidoo, named McDonald, a tall Scot, together with a barber, drove up in a buckboard. He asked me to go with them to Ballarat, which I consented to do. There was a man there called "Whiskers" who ran a saloon. No one knew where he came from or anything about him, but he was considered a good man to let alone. It was quite well known that Dr. McDonald and Whiskers had had some trouble, and the atmosphere grew rather tense on our arrival. This was my third year in that vicinity, and I was well known to most of the boys. After visiting two or three of the thirst emporiums, we walked into Whiskers' place.

Whiskers was there himself behind the bar. The Doctor knew a few of the men who were in the saloon and called them up to have a drink. I forgot to say that Whiskers wore a beautiful beard of chin whiskers which were very long; he was very proud of them.

When Whiskers was serving drinks directly in front of us, the Doctor picked a pair of shears out of the barber's pocket, reached out over the bar, took a good hold of the whiskers, and with one clip of the shears cut them off. Laying them on the bar with his left hand he said: "Here's your whiskers."

Whiskers' hand flew to his chin. For a few seconds everything was quiet, and I think nearly every man's hand in the room went toward his gun. Whiskers dropped his eyes on the bar and stared at the beard lying there; then someone gave a little laugh, and Whiskers looked up at the Doctor saying: "Doctor, the drinks are on the house." I presume he felt the same satisfaction as people do who have fought a good fight and lost. As far as I know, from that time on they were good friends.

There were a few small skunks on the desert that were spotted down the back, and to some degree resembled an ear of corn. They were called "hydrophobia skunks" and were supposed to be very poisonous. They had a habit of biting you while you were asleep, usually on the nose or on the finger. I have known their bite to be fatal. There were also a good many diamondback rattlesnakes, and a sprinkling of sidewinders which strike without coiling.

The sidewinder snake made a very peculiar track in the dust. It was very much like the track of the old-style steam tractor, little straight marks about two inches apart and about a foot long, side by side and open at the ends. Unless the dust was deep you could not tell which way he was going, he turned so short.

Some very wonderful sights could be seen from the rim of Death Valley during a storm. I have seen whirlwinds (sand spouts), which resemble water spouts, come up from the bottom over the rim, which was five thousand feet. There would sometimes be dozens of the spouts and the valley would look like a boiling caldron of sand. Some of them reached over the rim and a flourlike dust would spread out over all the country and would get into everything. It would be days in settling.

The smallest mine that I have ever known of was near Rhyolite, Nevada, and was called the Bullfrog. There was less than a wheelbarrowful of ore in it, but the ore was a beautiful green quartz which was sprinkled full of free gold and took a good polish. Most of it was made into jewelry—

stickpins, rings, and so forth. Shorty Harris was the discoverer.

I turned into the lower end of the main street of Rhyolite one day, coming from Death Valley. I was riding a burro and driving three others. A man was shot dead in the street about one hundred feet ahead of me. I pushed the burros on up the street. When I had gotten pretty well uptown another man was shot down on the sidewalk just opposite me. I began to think I was catching up with old times in Kansas. It occurred to me that Rhyolite might make a good camp after all.

In Goldfield at that time was the Great Northern bar, which was about one hundred feet long. With customers six or eight deep at the bar together with roulette, faro, Klondike, crap games, and poker tables, the place was rumored to be doing a fifty-thousand-dollar-a-day business. I don't know about that, but it was some camp, and you had to watch your step.

While in Rhyolite, at this time, I made some examinations of prospects for some prospective purchasers from the East. I was paid one hundred dollars per day for my services. I also made my employer some money. I found the prospects salted and turned them down. It was to have been a fifty-thousand-dollar cash deal. I was offered ten thousand dollars by the owners for a favorable report, but I could not see it that way.

I have cached water along the trail and when coming to it in a month, more or less, would find it rotten and not fit to drink. The same water will be perfectly clear and fresh and as good as it ever was if left to stand another month or so. I have had water at my camp in barrels go through the same performance.

If your burros bother you around camp and you want

to get rid of them for a while, this is a good way to do it: Pick a time when they are standing near camp looking at you. Pick up a pack saddle, look it over a little, lay it to one side. Take a saddle blanket, shake it out, and place it with the saddle. Drag over a couple of pack bags and look suspiciously once in a while at the burros. Act as though you are getting ready to break camp. In a very short time the burros will ease away, and you won't see anything of them for two or three days. It is very hard to get a burro to drink poisoned water. Thus, if the burro drank the water, it was good enough for me, even if I did have to strain out the dead mountain rats and a few birds.

I sent one of my Indian packers to Ballarat with burros for a load of groceries. On his return I checked him up and he was short a lot of corn beef. I spoke to him about it. "How you know?" he asked. I said: "The paper told me." On returning from the next trip for groceries, he was again short on corn beef. I accused him of taking it. He said: "No, no, paper no see'um." He put the paper inside of his shirt while he ate the beef.

The prospector is a peculiar sort of person. He was born that way, i.e., with a desire to be in faraway places with exposure and hard trips, and a thirst for hooch. I believe if a strike were reported at the North Pole he would be there in numbers, before the end of the first season, staking out his claims.

No matter whether his claims are of low-or high-grade ore, he generally salts them to make them appear richer. The ways of salting a ledge or cropping of ore are numerous. I have known a prospector to load his burrow with a high-grade ore from some mine or with high-grade float rock from some claims and pack it long distances to his ground where he fixes it in a way that he thinks it will get into the samples of some mining engineer whom he expects to induce to come out and examine his prospect. Sometimes he dissolves fine gold in a mixture of acids called "aqua regia." This he sprinkles on all exposed rocks on his claim.

Nearly all prospectors at some time or other have made rich strikes and have sold them for considerable money, but very few have ever kept the money long. They are not happy until it's gone. They want to be in the hills on a grubstake.

The prospector knows how to make simple tests for different kinds of metals, and is usually good with a gold pan or horn spoon. He is fairly honest except when talking about the richness of his claims. He will share his last bit of grub or water with you, and he knows what a burro is thinking about. Time doesn't mean much to him. If he does not strike it this year, that's all right; maybe he will next year. He is always planning to go back home when he makes a strike, but seldom gets by the first hog ranch.

A "hog ranch" was a wide place in the road about forty miles from nowhere with a saloon and a house where you could drink, eat, and sleep. The stagecoach passed about twice a week and freight teams made it a campground. Music was furnished by a phonograph. A girl or two were usually sticking around; they would teach you how to dance until your bank roll was gone.

A quartz-mining claim in the valley was six hundred feet wide and fifteen hundred feet long. You could locate and stake out as many claims as you wanted to. The discovery monument was usually a rock pyramid built six to eight feet high at an outcropping of the vein, where you had made the first discovery. Your notice of location, which you would write out on paper and put in the rock pile, generally in a tobacco can or between two flat stones, would read about like this:

> This Claim No. 1 will be known as the "Wild Cat"; beginning at this monument and going in an easterly direction for three hundred feet, thence northerly for fifteen hundred feet, thence westerly for six hundred feet, thence southerly for fifteen hundred feet, thence easterly for three hundred feet to point of beginning. Claim No. 2, etc., etc., etc. . . . .

You were supposed to record your claim within twenty days after location. All mining claims not patented ground, that the assessment work had not been done on, became delinquent at twelve o'clock midnight on New Year's Eve and could be relocated or jumped by anyone. This relocating would sometimes cause trouble and hard feelings.

Prospectors sometimes showed a little humor. I stopped one day at a newly made claim monument on the desert. The location notice read like this:

> This claim will be known as "Hot Air" claim. The boundaries are three hundred feet in an easterly direction and three hundred feet in a westerly direction. Then fifteen hundred feet straight up. Now, you son of a b——, jump it.

CHAPTER TWENTY-THREE

BALLARAT

IT DOES NOT SEEM RIGHT to leave the desert without a few lines about Ballarat and its inhabitants. The small adobe town lay on the east side of the Panamint Valley and up against the west slope of the Panamint Mountains, about seventy miles from Johannesburg. A stage line gave twice-a-week service, and there were freight teams at irregular intervals. Following the heyday of Old Panamint City, which was some miles to the northeast, Ballarat was the next boom camp in that district.

The Argus Range was on the west side of the valley. The valley was a series of dry salt and alkali flats. From the top of the Argus Range, fourteen miles across the valley, the little town of Ballarat was about the most Godforsaken-looking place you would ever see. The few little flat adobe buildings could just be made out through a dry atmosphere, where fourteen miles looked like three or four. The view from the west always gave me a depressing feeling; it looked like the "jumping-off place" of the world.

Your welcome was always good when you got to Ballarat. The boys of the surrounding hills were loyal to their town, and whenever one of them sold his claims or prospects, no matter whether it was for a few or many thousand dollars, he seldom got past Ballarat. He remained there until the last dollar was gone. Sobering up, he would be perfectly satisfied to go back to the hills.

Ballarat had been about the wildest gold boom town in that area; but by my time it had shrunk to about six saloons, two houses where you could get something to eat and a place to sleep, one general store, and a couple of stone burro corrals. Before the boom it was known as Post Office Springs. Anyone coming in from the outside would leave the mail there under a rock for prospectors or others. Those passing by would look the mail over and take what they wanted. The springs were in among some mesquite bushes a short distance from where the town is now. The inhabitants can best be described by telling you about the first night I spent there: I had come in on the stage. It was just about sundown and I noticed a little commotion at one of the saloons. About fifteen of "the boys" had gathered in and around a small room in the back of the saloon where the only demimondaine of the town was stretched out on a canvas cot. The boys by this time of day were pretty well lit up, as was their daily custom.

The talk that reached my ears as I stood on the outer edge of the crowd was about like this: "It's too bad to see Old Babe pass out. She has surely been a good old girl. She told me she had a weak heart."

"Is that so! Here, Bill, go over to the store and fetch some strychnine."

"Yes, that's what she needs, strychnine is good for weak hearts."

I thought by this time if anybody was going to say a few kind words to Babe, that it had better be done pretty quickly.

I stepped up to the crowd saying: "Let me see the girl."
About then one big fellow looked around and saw I was a
stranger and he said in a loud voice: "Gangway, here comes
the doctor."

When I reached the side of the cot she certainly did look
bad; her face was about the color of chalk. And the heat
was fierce. After being called "the doctor," I tried to make
good and took charge of the situation. I opened her dress
for air, folded a couple of newspapers, and put some of the
boys to fanning her. I ordered some burlap sacks soaked
in water and hung up over the back door, where a very hot
wind was blowing. We moved her cot over in front of the
door. The wind blowing through the sacks, which were
kept wet, soon had the air fresh and cool. It was not long
until Babe opened her eyes and began to come out of it.
Everybody was feeling better now and the bar was doing a
good business. Thirty minutes later Babe was also taking
nourishment at the bar.

Babe had a little secret. When I started to take down her
hair, which was done up in a big mop on top of her head,
although she seemed to be unconscious, her hand went up
in protest. On closer examination I saw the poor girl was
wearing a wig. I never betrayed her.

The bar was about fifty feet long. I had gone to the back
end of the saloon to write a post card, as the stage carrying
mail left the next morning. I was writing (on the head of
a whisky barrel) when I heard a shot from a pistol and
at the same time a shower of dirt and dust fell over me. Just
over my head on the wall hung a Bock Beer sign with a
bullet hole through it. I looked up along the side of the bar,
and at the far end stood a big roughneck-looking hombre
with a smoking gun in his hand. I called to him saying:
"Old-timer, you aren't shooting in very good form tonight.

198

Wait until I finish my writing and I'll shoot with you for drinks for the house." He accepted and when I walked up to him he had two Colt pistols laid out on the bar and said: "Take your choice."

I picked up the one closest to me, which was a .44 single-action, and said: "Bring down the billy goat" (pointing to the sign), "You shoot first," which he did. The sign still hung there. Then I cut loose. I have said before that a pop shot will sometimes kill the devil. Well, I drove the nail into the adobe wall, and down fell the sign. After everybody had slacked his thirst, this hombre and I became good friends; in fact, a little later on we were partners in a group of claims called the "Tro-Jan," which we worked for some time. When together we never went to bed in the dark but always shot the candle out after getting in bed.

Shortly, after a few rounds of drinks (I am speaking still of my first night in Ballarat), my friend decided he would shoot at a lamp which hung over the bar at the far end of the room. Under the lamp stood the phonograph with a big horn. He missed the chimney of the lamp but hit the bowl which held about a half-gallon of kerosene. The glass, oil, and all fell into the phonograph, which didn't help the music for the rest of the night.

At three o'clock in the morning I locked up the saloon; everyone else was down and out including the proprietor. I put the keys in my pocket and went to my room to sleep in a bed which had sheets that were at one time white. When I lay down I jumped up as though I had sat on a hot stove. This may seem just a little far-fetched to a person who does not know the desert, but it's absolutely a fact. I had to ease onto that bed by degrees.

The general store had adobe walls and a dirt floor which was kept wet. In the center of the room stood a post on which hung a thermometer. During this stay in Ballarat, I never saw it register below 116° either night or day. No wonder the boys drank whisky.

Ballarat had no officers of the law and all the boys slept where they fell. It was a common sight about the middle of the morning to see one of them with a bucket of beer and a dipper, reviving the fallen ones sufficiently to get them into the shade of some adobe wall.

The last officer of the law who had served there as constable and policeman wore a metal badge on his vest, which was a mistake. One day one of the boys made a bet that he could shoot the officer's badge off without hurting him. They buried the poor fellow next morning. My friend and partner of the Tro-Jan group of claims was afterward put to death in Canada for a crime committed there.

I left California in 1910 and went to see my mother, who lived in Georgia. I had not been that far east since I was nineteen years old. I soon drifted into west Florida and have called that my home ever since.

of which *The West of the Texas Kid* is Number 20, was started in 1953 by the University of Oklahoma Press. It is designed to introduce today's readers to the exciting events of our frontier past and to some of the memorable writings about them. The following list is complete as of the date of publication of this volume:

1. Prof. Thomas J. Dimsdale. *The Vigilantes of Montana.* With an introduction of E. DeGolyer.
2. A. S. Mercer. *The Banditti of the Plains.* With a foreword by William H. Kittrell.
3. Pat F. Garrett. *The Authentic Life of Billy, the Kid.* With an introduction by Jeff C. Dykes.
4. Yellow Bird (John Rollin Ridge). *The Life and Adventures of Joaquín Murieta.* With an introduction by Joseph Henry Jackson.
5. Lewis H. Garrard. *Wah-to-yah and the Taos Trail.* With an introduction by A. B. Guthrie, Jr.
6. Charles L. Martin. *A Sketch of Sam Bass, the Bandit.* With an introduction by Ramon F. Adams.
7. Washington Irving. *A Tour on the Prairies.* With an introduction by John Francis McDermott.
8. *X. Beidler: Vigilante.* Edited by Helen Fitzgerald Sanders in collaboration with William H. Bertsche, Jr. With a foreword by A. B. Guthrie, Jr.
9. Nelson Lee. *Three Years among the Comanches.* With an introduction by Walter Prescott Webb.
10. *The Great Diamond Hoax and Other Stirring Incidents in the Life of Asbury Harpending.* With a foreword by Glen Dawson.
11. *Hands Up; or, Twenty Years of Detective Life in the*

Mountains and on the Plains: Reminiscences by General D. J. Cook, Superintendent of the Rocky Mountain Detective Association. With an introduction by Everett L. DeGolyer, Jr.

12. Will Hale. *Twenty-four Years a Cowboy and Ranchman in Southern Texas and Old Mexico.* With an introduction by A. M. Gibson.

13. Gen. James S. Brisbin, U.S.A. *The Beef Bonanza; or, How to Get Rich on the Plains.* With a foreword by Gilbert C. Fite.

14. Isabella L. Bird. *A Lady's Life in the Rocky Mountains.* With an introduction by Daniel J. Boorstin.

15. W. T. Hamilton. *My Sixty Years on the Plains.* With an introduction by Donald J. Berthrong.

16. *The Life of John Wesley Hardin, As Written by Himself.* With an introduction by Robert G. McCubbin.

17. Elizabeth Bacon Custer. *"Boots and Saddles"; or, Life in Dakota with General Custer.* With an introduction by Jane R. Stewart.

18. John F. Finerty. *War-Path and Bivouac; or, The Conquest of the Sioux.* With an introduction by Oliver Knight.

19. Frederic Remington. *Pony Tracks.* With an introduction by J. Frank Dobie.

20. Thomas Edgar Crawford. *The West of the Texas Kid.* Edited and with an introduction by Jeff C. Dykes.

202

UNIVERSITY OF OKLAHOMA PRESS

NORMAN

F
595
C89

Crawford, Thomas Edgar, 1867-1941.
   The West of the Texas Kid, 1881-1910; recollections of Thomas Edgar Crawford, cowboy, gun
fighter, rancher, hunter, miner. Edited and with
an introd. by Jeff C. Dykes. With original drawings by Nick Eggenhofer. [1st ed.]   Norman,
University of Oklahoma Press [1962]
   202p. illus.   20cm.   (The Western frontier
library, 20)

Edited from the manuscript dictated by the author in 1938, now published for the first time.

1.Frontier and pioneer life-The West. I.Dykes, Jefferson
Chenoweth, 1900-   ed.   II.Title.